Pâtisserie

MURIELLE VALETTE

Constable • London

Constable & Robinson Ltd
55–56 Russell Square
London WC1B 4HP
www.constablerobinson.com

First published in the UK by Constable,
an imprint of Constable & Robinson Ltd, 2013

A copy of the British Library Cataloguing in
Publication Data is available from the British Library

ISBN 978-1-9089-7413-6 (trade paperback)
ISBN 978-1-4721-1014-5 (ebook)

Printed and bound in the UK

1 3 5 7 9 10 8 6 4 2

Murielle Valette was born into a family of French chefs. She has been making and enjoying food for as long as she can remember. Learning the family tradition first, she was then classically trained and worked alongside the best chefs in France and the UK. After fifteen years of learning how to create *des Pâtisseries à la française*, she is now renowned for her unique combination of French-inspired cooking with English flavours and traditions. Head pastry chef at the Michelin-starred restaurant Ockenden Manor Hotel, south of London, Murielle dedicates her time and energy to sharing her passion for French pastry in the UK.

To Mamie, Jeanne Salvagnac (1922-2010),
my loving grandmother who introduced me to pâtisserie as a child.

Contents

Chapter 4 – Puff pastry   95

Chapter 5 – Choux pastry   115

Chapter 6 – Rising doughs

Chapter 7 – Flans, creams and egg batters

Chapter 8 – Sponge cakes   191

Chapter 9 – Sweet treats   219

Preface

This book is a tribute to passion: passion for pâtisserie and passion for France. It is a celebration of a French *art de vivre* and is intended for all Francophiles and chefs in the making. In this book you will find recipes that cover a whole range of exquisite pâtisserie – from family desserts to classic and traditional French pâtisserie. I want to share with you recipes from my childhood that I learnt from my Maman, who herself learnt from her mother.

A common misconception that surrounds French pâtisserie is that it is difficult to make. You will discover in this book the well-kept secrets of French pastry chefs; all classic French pâtisserie is built around a few basic techniques and core recipes. If you learn to master these, you can recreate any French dessert from the simplest to the most complicated. You will then be able to serve at home what you see in the pastry shops and bakeries or eat in the traditional restaurants and bistros in France.

I have cooked for as long as I can remember. This passion is still central to my life, both at home and at work. I aim to show that it is easy to bring the work of professional pastry chefs into every home. Everybody can learn how to bake French desserts if the recipes are explained properly. Following this book will hopefully be like taking a private pastry course at home.

In the richly illustrated first section, you will find many pictures explaining the basic techniques step by step. The main part of the book contains all the recipes, organized in chapters by pastry type. Most recipes will use one or several of the basic techniques explained at the beginning of the book. It also contains shortcuts and professional tips for successful and rapid pastry-making at home.

Et voilà! I hope this book will become your favourite companion in the kitchen and give you the pleasure of sharing amazing desserts with those you love.

Happy baking!

Murielle

The basic techniques

The most important thing when making French pâtisserie is a good pair of hands. Of course, electric mixers or food processors can be used to accelerate and simplify the work but ultimately everything can be done by hand. A hand whisk works just as well as an electric whisk, an electric paddle can be replaced by a spatula and the dough hook by your hands. Using your hands is a little bit more physical of course, but quite satisfying.

At work and at home I prefer to work on a marble or stone surface, but most surfaces will suffice as long as they are smooth and fairly cold. (If the work surface is warm, you can cool it down with ice cubes and wipe it dry.)

There are, however, a few pieces of cooking equipment that I would recommend you buy if you do not already have them at home:

- A sugar thermometer
- A blowtorch for caramelizing tarts and creams
- A couple of non-stick baking trays
- A silicone mat for cooking sponge and biscuits
- Piping bags with a set of nozzles to fill or decorate cakes

If you are contemplating buying new moulds, I recommend non-stick loose-bottom cake or tart tins. However, some recipes in the book, like savarins or madeleines, require the purchase of specific moulds.

The baking phase is as important as the making of the dessert. All ovens are different and you know your oven best. So, follow the cooking temperatures and times in this book but also keep a close eye on what is going on in the oven to ensure you get a good bake. Ideally, all pâtisseries should be cooked in a fan oven because the temperature inside the oven is evenly distributed. A static oven can also be used but it will require more care and eventually some adjustments of the temperature and the cooking time.

Sweet shortcrust pastry

LA PÂTE BRISÉE SUCRÉE

Ideal for cooked fruit and custard tarts, use non-fragile fruits like apples, pears, apricots, plums etc, with this pastry. The fruits and the shortcrust pastry can be cooked simultaneously.

For 500g of pastry / **Preparation time:** 15 minutes / **Resting time in fridge:** 1 hour

INGREDIENTS
250g plain flour
160g cold butter, diced
50ml milk, at room
  temperature
5g salt
15g caster sugar
1 medium egg yolk

BY HAND
1. Put the flour and diced butter onto a work surface.

2. Use your fingertips to coat each piece of butter with flour. Then, with both hands, work the mixture until it has a sandy texture.

3. Make a well and pour the milk into its centre. Add the salt and caster sugar and dissolve them in the milk by stiring using your fingertips. Finally, add the egg yolk.

4. Gradually incorporate the flour mix into the liquid, starting from the inside of the well.

5. When the liquid has disappeared, use both hands to mix the pastry until it has an even consistency. Do not overwork it – when all the ingredients are combined, it is ready.

6. Gather the pastry into a rectangular shape (3cm thick) to make it easier to roll out. Wrap in cling film and rest in the fridge for a minimum of 1 hour.

USING A FOOD PROCESSOR OR AN ELECTRIC MIXER WITH A PADDLE
At a slow speed, mix the flour, butter, caster sugar and salt until the mixture has a sandy texture. Add the milk and egg yolk, and mix until it has an even consistency(a few seconds is generally enough).

👍 GOOD TO KNOW
The resting time in the fridge is necessary. It relaxes the pastry, makes it easier to roll out and stops it from shrinking during cooking.

Sweet pastry

LA PÂTE SUCRÉE

This sweet pastry is sweeter than the sweet shortcrust pastry and mainly used for blind baked almond cream, flan and chocolate tarts.

For 500g of pastry / **Preparation time:** 15 minutes / **Resting time in the fridge:** 1 hour

[INGREDIENTS]
230g plain flour
1 small pinch of salt
140g cold butter, diced
1 medium egg
55g caster sugar

BY HAND
1. Put the flour, salt and diced butter onto the work surface.

2. Use your fingertips to coat each piece of butter with flour, then, with both hands, work the mixture until it has a sandy texture.

3. Make a well and put the egg and caster sugar in its centre.

4. Use your fingertips to mix the egg with the caster sugar, then incorporate the flour mix, starting at the inside of the well, until it has an even consistency. Do not overwork – when all the ingredients are combined, it is ready.

5. Gather the pastry into a rectangular shape (3cm thick) to make it easier to roll out. Wrap in cling film and rest in the fridge for a minimum of 1 hour.

USING A FOOD PROCESSOR OR AN ELECTRIC MIXER WITH A PADDLE
At slow speed, mix the flour, salt, caster sugar and butter until the mixture has a sandy texture. Add the egg and mix until it has an even consistency (a few seconds is generally enough). See the step-by-step photos on page 7 – the method is similar.

👍 GOOD TO KNOW

The sweet shortcrust pastry, the sweet pastry and the sablée recipes make 500g of pastry. For each 500g recipe, one egg is needed. A tart usually requires about 300g of pastry. Since it is difficult to divide an egg, I recommend the following little tip: as raw pastry can be frozen without damage, you can double the basic quantity of ingredients and divide the pastry into three parts. Keep one part in the fridge and freeze the other two for later use. When needed, defrost the pastry overnight in the fridge and it will be ready for use the following morning.

Sablée pastry

LA PÂTE SABLÉE

Crispy and crumbly, sablée pastry is used blind baked for fresh fruits, cream and chocolate tarts or tartlets.

For 500g of pastry / **Preparation time:** 15 minutes / **Resting time in the fridge:** 1 hour

[INGREDIENTS]
260g plain flour
1 small pinch of salt
120g icing sugar
120g cold butter, diced
1 medium egg

USING A FOOD PROCESSOR OR AN ELECTRIC MIXER WITH A PADDLE
See the step-by-step photos on page 7

1. At slow speed, mix the flour, salt, icing sugar and butter until the mixture has a sandy texture.

2. Add the egg.

3. Then mix until it has an even consistency (a few seconds is generally enough).

4. Gather the pastry into a rectangular shape (3cm high) and wrap it in clingfilm. Set in the fridge for a minimum of 1 hour.

BY HAND
See the step-by-step photos for the sweet pastry on page 9 – the method is similar.

1. Put the flour, salt, icing sugar and diced butter onto a work surface.

2. Use your fingertips to coat each piece of butter with the flour mix, then, with both hands, work the mixture until it has a sandy texture.

3. Make a well and add the egg to its centre.

4. Use your fingertips to rub the egg into the flour mix until it has an even consistency. Do not overwork – when all the ingredients are combined, it's ready.

5. Gather the pastry into a rectangular shape (3cm thick) to make it easier to roll out. Wrap it in cling film and rest in the fridge for a minimum of 1 hour.

Puff pastry

Flaky pastry or rough puff pastry are commonly used instead of puff pastry in Britain. They consist of diced butter combined with the dough and folded together instead of a block of butter folded inside the dough.

For 1.3kg of pastry / Preparation time: 40 minutes / **Resting time in the fridge:** 2¹/₂ hours

INGREDIENTS
400g plain flour
100g white bread flour (T55)
10g salt
300ml water
1 teaspoon white wine vinegar

500g cold butter (2 x 250g packs)

Make the dough
BY HAND

1. Sift the plain flour and the white bread flour onto the work surface and make a well in the centre.

2. Add the salt, water and white wine vinegar. (The vinegar will stop the pastry from turning grey after 24 hours in the fridge.)

3. Using your fingertips, gradually incorporate the flour, starting from the inside of the well.

4. When the mixture thickens, use your hands to bring it together until it forms a dough.

5. Form a ball without kneading. Cover the dough in cling film and store in the fridge for 30 minutes.

Preparing the butter
See step-by-step photos in croissant dough recipe (steps 5 and 6), page 17.

6. Lay out 2 pieces of cling film (40 x 60cm) on top of each other on the work surface.

7. Put the butter in the middle and fold over the cling film, leaving a gap between the butter and the edge of the cling film to allow the butter to spread. Use a rolling pin to make a square 1cm thick.

8. Store flat in the fridge for 30 minutes.

Folding the pastry (6 folds)
9. Remove the butter from the fridge and leave it to warm up for 15 minutes. On a floured work surface, roll out the dough into a large square (40 x 40cm) and put the butter into its centre (see diagram 1a opposite).

10. Wrap the butter by folding over the corners of the dough as shown in diagram 1b below.

Diagram 1

Folding the pastry (6 folds)

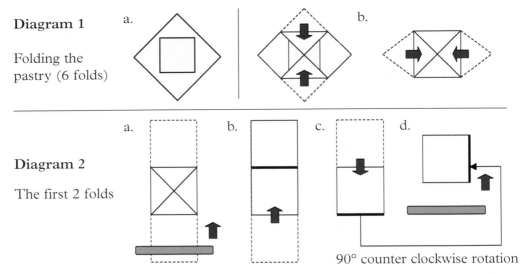

a.   b.

a.   b.   c.   d.

Diagram 2

The first 2 folds

90° counter clockwise rotation

The first 2 folds (see diagram 2a above).

11. On a floured work surface, roll out to form a rectangle that measures 30 x 60cm.

12. Remove excess flour with a brush or the palm of your hands. Fold the bottom section of the pastry into the middle (see diagram 2b above).

13. Then fold the top third on top (see diagram 2c above).

14. Rotate the pastry 90° counter-clockwise (see diagram 2d above). You've made the first fold.

15. Repeat steps 11 to 14 to make the second fold.

16. Mark the top right corner with two fingerprints. It will help you remember how many folds you have made. Wrap the pastry in cling film to prevent it drying out and place in the fridge for 30 minutes.

The 3rd and 4th folds

17. Take the pastry out of the fridge and place it on the floured work surface with the opening (marked in black in the drawing) on your right-hand side. This will ensure that you do not undo the fold you made earlier. Repeat the process for the first 2 folds.

18. Mark the top-right corner with 4 fingerprints and wrap it in cling film. Put the pastry in the fridge for 30 minutes.

The 5th and 6th folds

19. Take the pastry out of the fridge and place it on the floured work surface with the opening on your right-hand side. Repeat the process for the first two folds again.

20. Wrap the pastry in cling film and place it in the fridge for 30 minutes before use.

Choux pastry

Choux pastry is used in the making of individual pastries like Chantilly choux, éclairs or profiteroles and also family cakes like Paris-Brest, Saint-Honoré or croquembouche.

Makes 60 large choux or 40 éclairs (700g of pastry) / **Preparation time:** 20 minutes
Baking time: 15–20 minutes at 200°C/400°F/Gas Mark 6 + 15–20 minutes at 160°C/325°F/Gas Mark 3 to dry out. (The baking time will change according to the size of the pieces.)

INGREDIENTS
250ml water
100g butter, diced
5g salt
12g caster sugar
125g white bread flour, sifted
4 medium eggs

1 beaten egg, to glaze

BY HAND
1. In a saucepan, bring the water, diced butter, salt and sugar to the boil until the water and melted butter are combined.

2. Take the saucepan off the heat and add all the flour. With a spatula, stir gently at first, then vigorously, until the flour is fully incorporated.

3. Put the saucepan back on the hob, at medium heat, to dry out the mix. Keep stirring for about 30 seconds until the mixture is no longer sticking to the saucepan and the spatula.

4. Pour the mix into a large bowl and stir in the eggs one at a time with a spatula. (This step can also be done with an electric mixer fitted with a paddle.)

5. To check the consistency of the mixture, take out some pastry with the tip of the spatula: the end of the pastry should slide back down and form a peak still attached to the spatula.

6. Fill a piping bag fitted with a large nozzle and use the dough straight away. On non-stick trays, pipe the choux or éclairs in staggered rows.

7. Dip a fork or a pastry brush in the beaten egg and use to level out the pastry.

8. Place a ramekin filled with 1cm of boiling water at the bottom of the oven and bake the choux pastry in the centre. The first 15 minutes of baking must be done with the oven door closed at all times to avoid the risk of the choux pastry collapsing.

⌁ GOOD TO KNOW

This small amount of pastry will make a lot of choux. You can either divide the recipe in half or make it all and freeze any excess. The mixture can be piped onto greaseproof paper and frozen raw for later use.

Croissant dough

LA PÂTE À CROISSANTS

The croissant dough is made the same way as the puff pastry. But the croissant dough is richer and only 4 folds are made. It can also be used to make almond croissants, pains au chocolat or pains aux raisins.

For 1.1kg of pastry / **Preparation time:** 45 minutes
Resting time in the fridge: overnight for the dough (12 hours) + 1 hour

INGREDIENTS
15g fresh yeast
275ml semi-skimmed or
   full fat milk, at room
   temperature
500g white bread flour
7.5g salt
75g caster sugar

250g cold butter

USING AN ELECTRIC MIXER FITTED WITH A DOUGH HOOK
The croissant dough can also be done by hand following the puff-pastry dough method on page 12

Make the dough (This step should be done the day before)
1. Dissolve the fresh yeast in the milk.

2. Put the flour, salt and caster sugar into the mixing bowl.

3. Turn the mixer on at a slow speed, then slowly pour in the milk mixture. Mix for 5 minutes until the dough starts to come unstuck from the bowl.

4. Remove the dough from the mixing bowl and place it in a lightly oiled bowl. Cover with cling film and leave to rest overnight in the fridge.

Prepare the butter (This step should also be done the day before)
5. Lay out 2 pieces of cling film (40 x 60cm) on top of each other on the work surface. I use 2 pieces of film because one is simply not enough and you risk tearing the cling film. Put the butter in the middle.

6. Fold over the cling film, leaving a gap between the butter and the edge of the cling film to allow the butter to spread. Use a rolling pin to make a square 1cm thick.

7. Store flat in the fridge for 30 minutes.

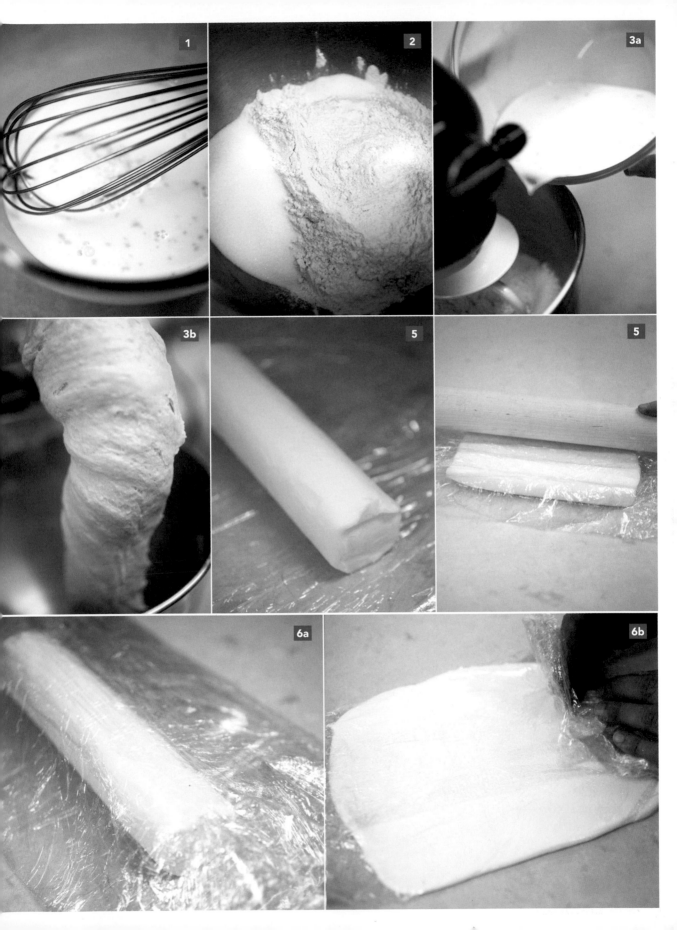

Folding the dough (4 folds)

8. The following day, remove the butter from the fridge and leave it to warm up for 15 minutes.

9. Turn over the dough on a lightly floured work surface and remove the fermentation gas, pressing on the dough with the palms of your hands without kneading (kneading the dough will give it some elasticity and make it harder to roll).

10. Shape the dough into a square and roll out the 4 corners, leaving the middle untouched.

11. Flatten the middle of the dough with your hands or using the rolling pin, and place the butter in the centre.

12. Wrap the butter up by covering it with the 4 sides of the dough.

The first 2 folds (See diagram 2 for the puff pastry, page 13)

13. On a floured work surface, roll out the dough into a long rectangle (40 x 60cm). Remove the excess flour with a brush or the palm of your hand.

14. Fold the bottom section of the dough onto the middle section.

15. Then fold the top third over the top and press down the edges.

16. Make a 90° counter-clockwise rotation of the dough. You've just made the first fold.

17. Repeat steps 13 to 16 to make the second fold.

18. Mark the top-right corner with two fingerprints. It will help you remember how many folds you have made. Wrap the dough in cling film to prevent it drying out and put it in the fridge for 30 minutes.

The 3rd and 4th folds

19. Remove the pastry from the fridge and place it on a floured work surface with the opening on your right-hand side. This will ensure that you do not undo the fold you made earlier. Repeat steps 13 to 17 to make 2 more folds.

20. Mark the top right corner with 4 fingerprints and wrap the dough in cling film. Put it in the fridge for 30 minutes before use.

👍 GOOD TO KNOW

The resting time overnight in the fridge allows the dough to prove (rise) and develop more flavour. The yeast will not make the dough rise right away, especially if placed in the fridge: it needs at least 1 or 2 hours at room temperature or overnight in the fridge for the dough to double up in size. The yeast feeds itself on sugars present in the starch of the flour. As a result, it converts the sugars into carbon dioxide and ethanol, which makes the dough rise. That alcoholic fermentation changes the taste of the dough and will bring more flavours to the final product.

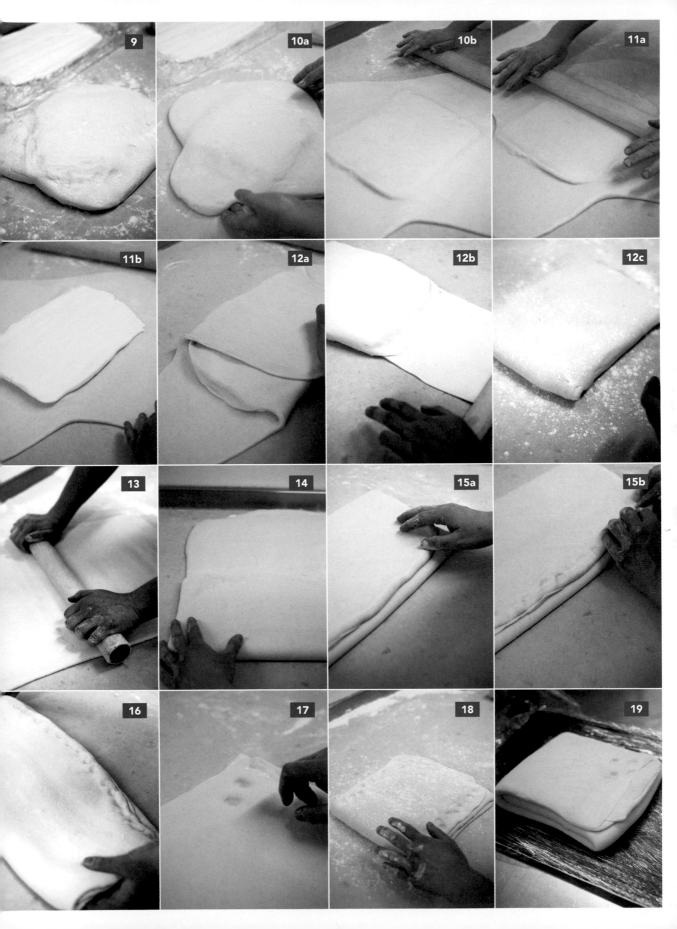

Brioche dough

LA PÂTE À BRIOCHE

The brioche dough is a rising dough. It is light and slightly sweet. It can be shaped into many different forms and hold all sorts of flavours (pink praline, chocolate or mixed peel).

Makes 600g of dough / **Preparation time:** 20 minutes / **Proving time:** 2–3 hours in a warm place or overnight in fridge / **Resting time:** 1¹/₂ hours in the fridge (if proved in a warm place first)

INGREDIENTS
10g fresh yeast
25ml semi-skimmed or
   full fat milk, at room
   temperature
250g white bread flour
   (T55)
5g salt
12g caster sugar
3 small eggs, at room
   temperature (150g)
125g soft butter

USING AN ELECTRIC MIXER FITTED WITH A DOUGH HOOK
The step-by-step photos are for a double recipe, the paddle is more appropriate for a single recipe

1. Dissolve the fresh yeast in the milk.

2. Put the flour, salt, caster sugar and eggs into the bowl of the mixer.

3. Add the milk and yeast, and work the mix for 10 minutes at slow speed.

4. Incorporate the soft butter and work the dough until it has an even consistency and comes unstuck from the surface of the bowl.

5. With kitchen paper, grease a large bowl with little oil (olive or vegetable). Place the dough in the middle and cover the bowl with a wet cloth or cling film, then continue with either method 1 or 2 below.

6. **Method 1** – The brioche dough can be made the day before use. After covering it, place it in the fridge and leave to prove slowly overnight. The following day, turn over the dough on a floured work surface and remove the fermentation gas by pressing on the dough with the palms of your hands (without kneading). The dough is now ready to use.
Method 2 – Prove the dough in a warm place (20–25°C) until it doubles in size (2–3 hours depending of the temperature of the ingredients and the room). Remove the fermentation gas by folding it on a floured work surface. Put the dough back in the bowl, cover and put in the fridge for a minimum of 1¹/₂ hours before use.

THE BRIOCHE MIX IS QUITE WET AND STICKY BUT CAN BE MADE BY HAND
Dissolve the fresh yeast in the milk. On a work surface, sift the flour, salt and sugar. Make a well and put the eggs then the milk and fresh yeast mix into its centre. With your fingertips, mix the liquids

together, then gradually incorporate the flour starting from the middle of the well. Gather the mixture together and work it with both hands by stretching it up and down on the work surface to give it some elasticity. Finally, spread out the dough on the work surface using your fingertips (20 x 30cm) and distribute the diced soft butter. Incorporate it by folding the dough over the butter and pushing it down. Repeat this action several times until there is an even consistency. Then, follow steps 5 and 6.

👍 GOOD TO KNOW

Fresh yeast is fragile; if it makes direct contact with the salt or sugar it will die and become inactive. When added to the dough mixture, the yeast must be combined straight away. Paradoxically, sugar combined with liquid (milk or water) can be used to activate the yeast if only left in contact for a short period of time.

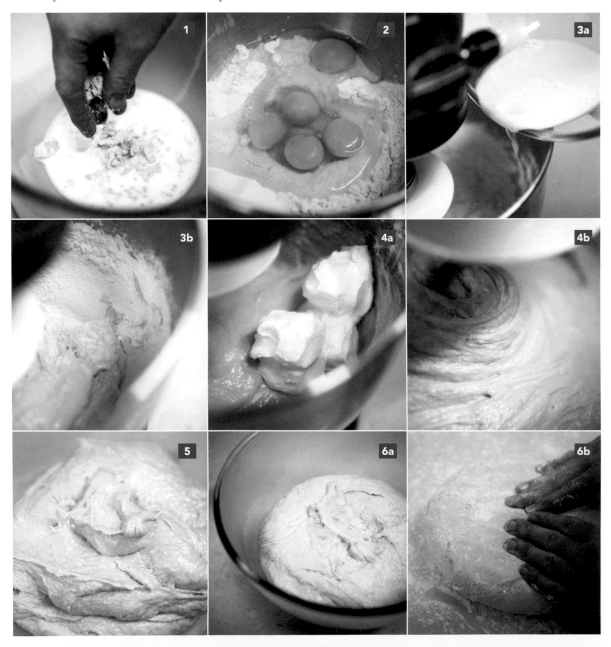

Savarin dough

The savarin dough is wet and sticky. It's used in the making of babas and savarins. After baking they are light and dry, and are then soaked in a syrup usually flavoured with a spirit such as rum or kirsch.

Makes 1 large (18cm) or 16 individual savarins (7cm) (500g of dough) / **Preparation time:** 20 minutes / **Proving time:** 1 hour / **Baking time:** For a large savarin, 30–40 minutes at 180°C/350°F/Gas Mark 4 / For individual savarins, 10–12 minutes at 200°C/400°F/Gas Mark 6

INGREDIENTS
10g fresh yeast
50ml semi-skimmed or
  full fat milk, at room
  temperature
225g white bread flour
5g salt
20g caster sugar
$2^{1}/_{2}$ medium eggs
50g soft butter

WITH AN ELECTRIC MIXER FITTED WITH A DOUGH HOOK
The step-by-step photos are for a double recipe, the paddle is more appropriate for a single recipe.

1. Dissolve the fresh yeast in the milk

2. Put the flour, salt, sugar and eggs into the mixing bowl. Add the milk and yeast, and work the mix for 10 minutes at slow speed.

3. Add the soft butter and continue to work the dough for a couple of minutes at the same speed, until it comes unstuck from the surface of the bowl.

4. Grease the savarin mould(s) with butter and flour. Remove the excess flour by knocking the mould(s) on the work surface.

5. Fill the mould(s) with dough to one-third using a teaspoon, tablespoon or a piping bag fitted with a medium-sized nozzle.

6. Leave to rise in a warm place (25–35°C) for about 1 hour until the dough doubles in size.

7. Bake the savarin(s), checking on them while cooking, until they are evenly golden brown. Turn out and cool on a wire rack to avoid condensation.

THE DIFFERENCE BETWEEN BABAS AND SAVARINS
Babas and savarins are made from the same dough and both are soaked in a syrup. Babas can contain raisins, but on the whole it's their different shapes that determine what they are called. Savarins are a crown shape and are generally served with fruits, crème pâtissière or Chantilly cream. Babas are cooked in individual cylinders and normally served with whipped cream.

Génoise sponge

LA PÂTE À GÉNOISE

Extremely light and butter-free, the génoise sponge is used to make different kinds of cakes or gateaus. But it can simply be enjoyed on its own, with a homemade crème anglaise and a strawberry salad.

Makes 500g / Preparation time: 20 minutes
Baking time: 25–30 minutes at 160°C/325°F/Gas Mark 3

INGREDIENTS
4 medium eggs
125g caster sugar
seeds of 1 vanilla pod
(optional)
125g plain flour, sifted

BY HAND WITH A WHISK OR WITH AN ELECTRIC MIXER FITTED WITH A WHISK ATTACHMENT

1. Grease a 20cm cake tin with butter and dust with flour. Turn it over and knock it on the work surface to remove excess flour.

2. In a large bowl, whisk the eggs with the caster sugar (and the vanilla seeds if used) for 1–2 minutes until the mixture starts to whiten.

3. Put the bowl over a bain-marie (see box) and whisk vigorously by hand without stopping until the mix reaches 40–45°C (the temperature of a hot bath). Use a thermometer or your fingertip to check.

4. Remove the bowl from the bain-marie and pour the warm egg and caster-sugar mixture into the bowl of an electric mixer, if using. Make a sabayon by whisking at maximum speed for 10–15 minutes, until the mix cools down and thickens. This step can also be done by hand.

5. By hand with a spatula, combine the flour with the sabayon in 4 or 5 additions. This will help to avoid lumps without overworking the sponge.

6. Fill the mould with the mixture and bake the génoise straight away. Turn out and cool on a wire rack to avoid condensation.

How to make a bain-marie

On the hob: Fill a large saucepan with 3cm of water. Bring it up to 80°C; the water should be simmering, not boiling. Place a heatproof bowl on top of the saucepan without touching the water beneath. A bain-marie like this is used to slowly melt chocolate or to warm up an egg mix.

In the oven: Baking in a bain-marie is a technique used for cooking a crème brûlée, a crème caramel or egg whites inside a tray (5cm depth) filled with boiling water (2cm). The temperature of the oven can vary between 110°C/225°F/Gas Mark ¼ for a crème brûlée to 180°C/350°F/Gas Mark 4 for the floating islands' egg whites. With this technique, you can bake a crème brûlée, crème caramel or poach an egg white slowly. However, the baking must be controlled as it is possible to overcook the creams or egg whites.

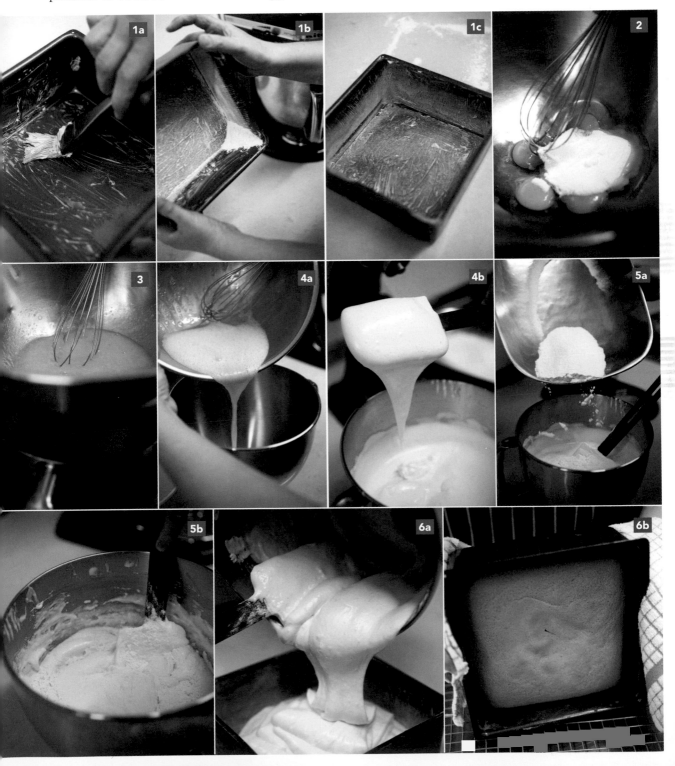

Crème anglaise

Crème anglaise is the French version of an English custard. It can be served cold or warm with a pudding, a cake or a fruit salad; it can also be churned to make an ice cream or used to make desserts like floating islands or bavarois creams.

Serves: 8–10 (400g of cream) / **Preparation time:** 15 minutes / **Cooking time:** 5 minutes
Cooling time: 30 minutes

INGREDIENTS

4 egg yolks
55g caster sugar
125ml full fat or semi-
  skimmed milk
175ml fresh double
  cream
1 vanilla pod (opened
  and scraped) or 1
  teaspoon of vanilla
  extract

BY HAND WITH A WHISK OR WITH AN ELECTRIC MIXER FITTED WITH A WHISK ATTACHMENT

1. Put the egg yolks and caster sugar into a large bowl and whisk for 3 minutes.

2. In a saucepan, bring to the boil the milk, double cream and vanilla pod and seeds, stirring occasionally.

3. While whisking, pour half the boiling liquid on top of the egg mix, starting with a small quantity to stop the yolk from coagulating.

4. Transfer the mixture back to the pan while stirring.

5. Cook the crème anglaise over a medium heat to 85°C. Stir with a spatula by making a figure of 8 shape; the white foam will disappear. If you don't have a thermometer you will know it is ready when the cream is thick enough to leave a finger mark on the spatula.

6. Pour the cream into a bowl through a very fine sieve.

7. Stop it cooking by placing the bowl of crème anglaise into another larger bowl filled with iced water, and stir for 30 seconds. Cool at room temperature for 30 minutes then cover with cling film and keep in the fridge.

👍 GOOD TO KNOW

Once the egg yolks and sugar are both in a bowl, mix together right away. This will prevent the yolks from coagulating and forming lumps.

If the cream reaches a temperature higher than 85°C, it might start to curdle. If this happens, the crème anglaise can be brought back together by whisking it energetically over a bowl filled with iced water.

Crème pâtissière

The crème pâtissière is a thick custard used in French pâtisserie to fill tarts, cakes and pastries. It can be plain or be flavoured with vanilla, coffee, chocolate, Grand Marnier or praline, for example.

Makes 450g of cream / **Preparation time:** 15 minutes / **Cooking time:** 5 minutes
Resting time in the fridge: 2 hours

INGREDIENTS
4 egg yolks
50g caster sugar
25g plain flour
350ml full fat or semi-skimmed milk
1 vanilla pod (opened and scraped) or 1 teaspoon of vanilla extract

BY HAND WITH A WHISK OR WITH AN ELECTRIC MIXER FITTED WITH A WHISK ATTACHMENT

1. Put the egg yolks and sugar into a large bowl and whisk for 3 minutes. Add the flour and whisk to combine.

2. In a saucepan, bring to the boil the milk with the vanilla pod and seeds, stirring occasionally.

3. Remove the pan from the heat, pour the egg mixture on top of the boiling liquid and stir with a hand whisk.

4. Put the mixture on the heat and bring to the boil at medium heat. Whisking in a figure of 8 shape, cook the crème pâtissière for 1 minute at the same temperature once it starts to boil, to cook off the flour.

5. Pour the cream into a large bowl through a very fine sieve (use a large bowl because the crème needs to cool down quickly).

6. Put a layer of cling film over the top, in direct contact with the surface of the cream to prevent the formation of a crust. Cool in the fridge for a minimum of 2 hours before use.

👍 GOOD TO KNOW

Use the crème pâtissière within 2 days, as after this it will start to lose its flavour.

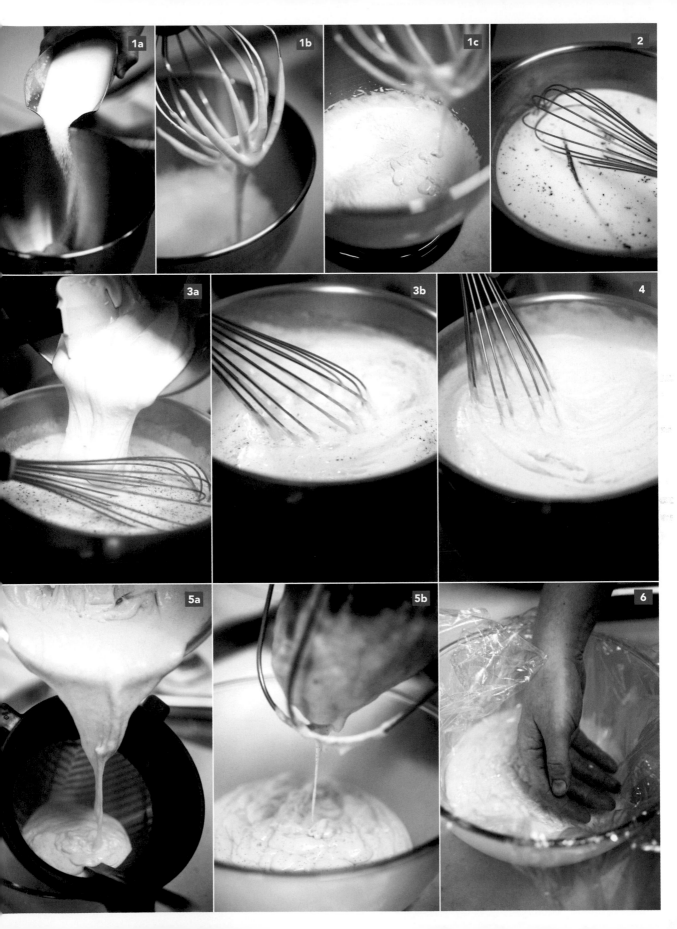

Almond cream

This almond cream is used to fill tarts or puff cakes and must be baked together with the pastry. Following the same method, the cream can be made with different sorts of nut powders such as pistachio or hazelnut.

Makes 420g of cream / **Preparation time:** 10 minutes

INGREDIENTS
90g ground almonds
25g plain flour
110g soft butter, diced
110g caster sugar
seeds of 1 vanilla pod or
   1 teaspoon of vanilla
   or almond extract
2 medium eggs

BY HAND WITH A SPATULA OR WITH AN ELECTRIC MIXER FITTED WITH A PADDLE

1. Sift together the ground almonds and plain flour.

2. In a mixing bowl, beat together the butter, sugar and vanilla seeds or extract until creamy.

3. Add the ground almonds and flour to the butter mixture and stir to combine.

4. Scrape the inside of the bowl with a spatula to bring the mix back together in the centre.

5. Add 1 egg, then smooth the mixture against the side of the bowl to avoid lumps. Add the second egg and combine well.

👍 GOOD TO KNOW

The almond cream will be easier to spread if used straight away. It can also be kept in the fridge but should be removed 30 minutes before use.

The vanilla pods, when only the seeds have been used like in the almond cream or the génoise sponge, can be kept and reused. For example, make a vanilla sugar by placing the vanilla pods in a jar with some caster or granulated sugar. You could also use them to flavour a syrup, a fruit compote or a cream.

Buttercream

French buttercream is made with a cooked sugar which makes it smooth, light and very creamy. It is used to fill cakes and pastries, and can be flavoured with vanilla, chocolate, spirits or nut paste.

Makes 550g of cream / **Preparation time:** 35 minutes / **Cooking time:** 5 minutes
You will need: a sugar thermometer or probe

INGREDIENTS
250g soft butter
1 medium egg
4 medium egg yolks
65g cold water
200g caster sugar
2 vanilla pods, opened
  and scraped (optional,
  according to each
  recipe)

WITH AN ELECTRIC MIXER FITTED WITH A WHISK
This recipe can also be done by hand following the same method.

1. With an electric mixer set at medium speed, work the butter until it is very soft and creamy. Alternatively, leave it out at room temperature 4 hours before making the buttercream.

2. In a mixing bowl, beat the egg and yolks for 1 minute.

3. Heat the water and sugar in a saucepan until 120°C. At this temperature the syrup must never be touched with bare hands and must be handled with great care.

4. Set the mixer at slow speed and pour the heated sugar onto the eggs without touching the whisk. Do not pour it too slowly or it will cool down and form sugar lumps. Turn the speed up and keep whisking until the mixture cools down. This step will take 15–20 minutes.

5. Flavour the cream with the vanilla seeds, if using.

6. When the mix has cooled, turn down the speed to low and add the very soft butter slowly to the mix, in 3 or 4 batches.

7. Finally, turn the speed back up to high for 30 seconds to make sure that all the ingredients are mixed well together.

👍 GOOD TO KNOW

With this type of cream, there is always the risk of the mixture curdling. If this does happen, you can save the cream by whisking it at a very high speed. If it doesn't come back together, place the buttercream in the fridge for 15 minutes if it's too warm, or warm up the bowl with a blowtorch or over a bain-marie (see page 24) for a few seconds if it's too cold, before whisking again. As a last resort, some extra soft butter can be added.

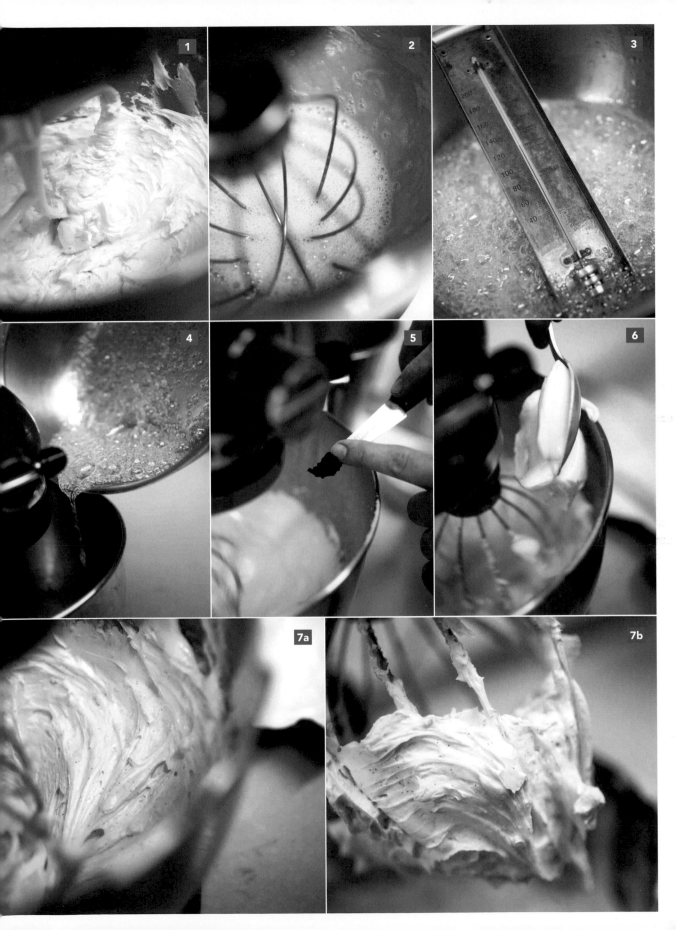

Chantilly cream

LA CRÈME CHANTILLY

This is a really easy and quick cream to make at the last minute. It can be served with a fruit salad or ice cream, or used to decorate a cake. It can also be poured on the top of a cup of coffee or hot chocolate.

Makes 300g of cream / **Preparation time:** 5 minutes

INGREDIENTS
280ml fresh double
    cream
20g caster sugar

BY HAND WITH A WHISK OR WITH AN ELECTRIC MIXER FITTED WITH A WHISK ATTACHMENT

1. Put the double cream in the fridge for 2 hours; it needs to be at a temperature of 4°C (cold from the fridge) in order for it to rise properly.

2. In a large bowl, whisk the cream at high speed in the electric mixer, or vigorously by hand, to incorporate some air.

3. When the cream starts to rise, sprinkle the caster sugar on the top.

4. Keep working the cream until it firms and forms a peak. Note that a softly whipped cream is called a whipped cream (photo 4a opposite); a firmly whipped cream is a Chantilly (photo 4b).

👍 GOOD TO KNOW

The Chantilly cream can be kept in the fridge for a few hours before it starts to collapse. After this, it might need to be whipped a second time before use.

34 *The basic techniques*

French meringue

A French meringue is made of uncooked caster sugar and egg whites. It's used in the making of cakes, creams or macaroons. The quantity of sugar can vary according to each recipe.

Makes 320g of meringue / **Preparation time:** 10 minutes

INGREDIENTS
3 egg whites (120g)
200g caster sugar

BY HAND WITH A WHISK OR WITH AN ELECTRIC MIXER FITTED WITH A WHISK ATTACHMENT

1. Whisk the egg whites at medium speed until they start to rise.

2. Gradually add the caster sugar, in 2 or 3 batches.

3. Whisk the meringue until it firms and forms a peak when you lift up the whisk (see page 37).

👍 GOOD TO KNOW

Egg whites can be kept for a few days in the fridge. I recommend you use at least 3-day-old egg whites (if you have them) when making a French meringue such as for a macaroon mix (see pages 226–232). The whipped egg whites will have more volume and the final mix will be lighter.

However, this doesn't apply to an uncooked mix made from French meringue like the Saint-Honoré cream (see page 130). In this case, the egg whites must be fresh and the mix should not be kept in the fridge for more than half a day.

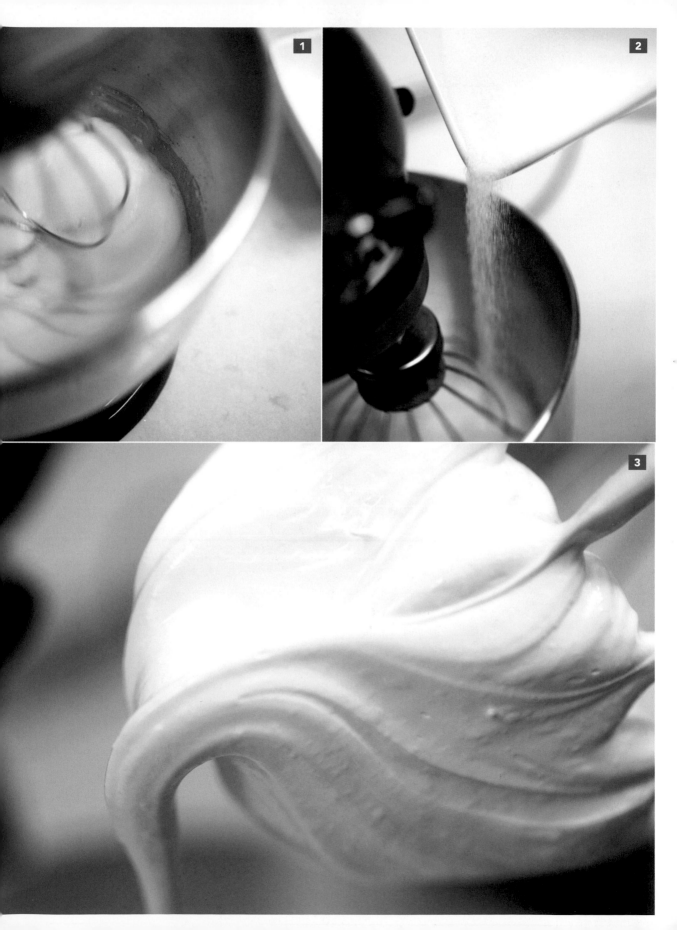

Italian meringue

LA MERINGUE ITALIENNE

An Italian meringue is made of cooked sugar poured on top of whipped egg whites. The cooked sugar will partially cook the egg whites, and makes it less fragile than a French meringue.

Makes 320g meringue / **Preparation time:** 15 minutes / **Cooking time:** 5 minutes
You will also need: A sugar thermometer or probe is necessary for this recipe

INGREDIENTS
170g caster sugar
85ml water
3 egg whites (120g)

BY HAND WITH A WHISK OR WITH AN ELECTRIC MIXER FITTED WITH A WHISK

1. In a saucepan, heat the caster sugar and water to 120°C. Check the temperature with a sugar thermometer or a probe. At this temperature the syrup must never be touched with bare hands and must be handled with great care.

2. Whisk the egg whites at medium speed until soft peaks form (see box). Set the mixer at a slow speed and pour the cooked sugar onto the eggs without touching the whisk. Do not pour it too slowly or it will cool down and form sugar lumps in the mix.

3. Whisk the meringue for a few minutes until it starts to cool and form a peak. Use straight away.

GOOD TO KNOW

Whisking egg whites, either when making a cake or a meringue, must always be done at medium speed: the air bubbles inside the whipped egg whites will be more even and less fragile when you combine them with other ingredients.

The stages of beaten egg whites

No peaks: The egg whites are foamy but not beaten enough to hold on to the whisk.

Soft peak: The peaks are just starting to hold when you turn the whisk upside down, but they will melt back down after a few seconds.

Peak or firm peak: The beaten egg whites hold firmly on a whisk turned upside down and the tip of the peak falls back down.

Stiff peak: The tip of the peak stands straight up on a whisk turned upside down.

Overbeaten: The egg whites will become grainy and collapse back on themselves. They can be used but it will show: the mix will stay grainy and it will not rise very well.

CHAPTER 1

Sweet shortcrust pastry

LA PÂTE BRISÉE SUCRÉE

How to line a tart tin

(or tartlet tins)

1. Sprinkle some flour on the work surface and the pastry.

2. Roll out the pastry to a thickness of 3mm. Keep moving it to stop it sticking to the work surface, adding a little more flour if necessary.

3. Put the tart tin over the pastry and trim the excess with a knife. (For tartlet tins, use a small plate or a bowl turned upside down, slightly wider than the tin, and cut the pastry all the way around it with a knife.)

4. Check the thickness and the regularity of the pastry/pastries, and roll it out again if necessary.

5. Remove the excess flour on the top with a brush or with your fingertips. Fold the pastry over the rolling pin and unroll it upside down on top of the tart tin. (For the tartlet tin, brush the flour off on both sides of the pastry bases and place them over the tartlet tins.)

6. Lower the pastry into the tin, then gently press it into the edges with your fingertips to line the base and sides.

7. Gather together the leftover pastry to form a small ball, coat it with flour and press along the side of the tart case to secure its position. (Proceed the same way with the tartlet bases.)

8. Remove the excess pastry with a knife or a rolling pin.

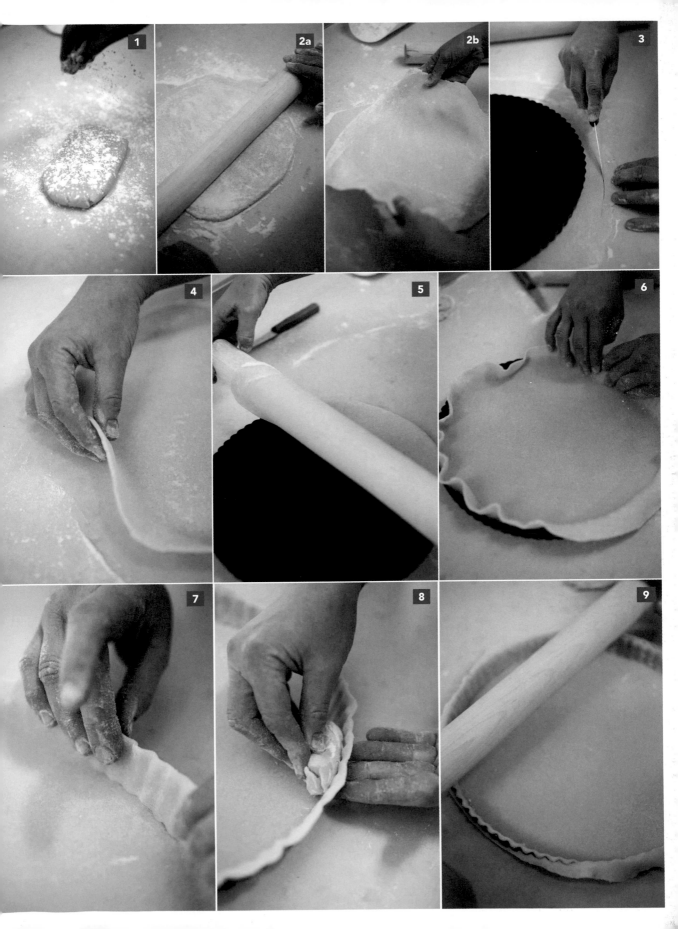

Apple and cinnamon tart

TARTE AUX POMMES ET À LA CANNELLE

There is something timeless about apple and cinnamon, I just love it. This tart is simple and delicious; it's the perfect Sunday lunch dessert for all the family.

Serves 10 (28cm tart) / **Preparation time:** 1 hour
Baking time: 1–1 hour 10 at 180°C/350°F/Gas Mark 4 / **You will need a 28cm tart tin**

INGREDIENTS
500g sweet shortcrust
   pastry (see page 6)

For the apple compote
3 medium Bramley
   apples
20g butter
100–120g caster sugar,
   to taste
50ml water
1 cinnamon stick or $^1/_2$
   teaspoon ground
   cinnamon

For the apple topping
6–8 Cox (or Braeburn)
   apples
$^1/_2$ lemon

For the glaze
20g butter
40g clear honey
1 pinch of ground
   cinnamon

1. Make the sweet shortcrust pastry and rest in the fridge for 1 hour.

2. Meanwhile, peel, core and dice the Bramley apples. In a pan set over a low heat, make a compote with the diced apples, butter, sugar, water and cinnamon stick or ground cinnamon. Bring to the boil and stir regularly. Simmer for 15 minutes until the fruits are cooked. Cool at room temperature.

3. Peel, cut in half and core the Cox or Braeburn apples. Put them in a bowl, squeeze over a few drops of lemon juice and mix by hand.

4. Roll out the shortcrust pastry to 4mm thick and line the tart tin (see page 42). Spread the cold compote over the base, cut the apple halves into 2mm slices and use to garnish the tart in circles.

5. Bake the tart for 40–45 minutes, then cover it with foil to protect the fruits and continue baking for another 20–25 minutes. Remove the foil and cool the tart in the tin.

6. In a small saucepan set over a low heat, warm up the butter, clear honey and ground cinnamon. Glaze the tart with the warm mixture using a pastry brush.

My mother's rhubarb tart

TARTE À LA RHUBARBE DE MAMAN

My mother's rhubarb tart is a unique adventure for the rhubarb lover.
Attention, danger of addiction!

Serves 10 (28cm tart) / **Preparation time:** 30 + 20 minutes / **Resting time in the fridge:** 1 hour
Baking time: 1–1 hour 10 at 180°C/350°F/Gas Mark 4 / **You will need a 28cm tart tin**

INGREDIENTS
500g sweet shortcrust
  pastry (see page 6)
5g baking powder

For the filling
700g rhubarb
260g caster sugar
20ml milk

1. Make the shortcrust pastry following the method on page 6, mixing the baking powder with the flour. Rest in the fridge for 1 hour.

2. Wash, peel and cut the rhubarb into strips then into 2cm batons.

3. Roll out the pastry to a thickness of 4mm and use to line the tart tin (see page 42).

4. Cover the bottom of the pastry base with 120g of the caster sugar, add the rhubarb batons and sprinkle another 100g of caster sugar on top.

5. Gather the leftover pastry into a ball and roll it out to 3mm. Brush with a thin layer of milk, sprinkle over a little more sugar (40g) and cut out some strips to decorate the tart in a lattice pattern.

6. Bake the tart for 40–45 minutes, then cover with foil to protect the fruits and continue baking for another 20–25 minutes. Remove the foil and cool the tart in the tin.

✓ CHEF'S TOP TIP

This recipe can also be made with half the amount of rhubarb mixed with 2 diced Bramley apples.

Greengage tart

This recipe can be made with all kinds of plums (mirabelle, purple, red, Victoria) or stone fruits (apricots, peaches, cherries). The quantity of sugar needed will vary according to the acidity of the fruits. The more acid the fruit has the more sugar your tart will need.

Serves 10 (28cm tart) / **Preparation time:** 30 + 10 minutes / **Resting time in the fridge:** 1 hour
Baking time: 1–1 hour 10 at 180°C/350°F/Gas Mark 4 / **You will need a 28cm tart tin**

INGREDIENTS
500g sweet shortcrust
    pastry (see page 6)
5g baking powder

For the filling
700g greengages
90g caster sugar, to taste

1 egg yolk

1. Make the shortcrust pastry following the method on page 6, mixing the baking powder with the flour. Rest in the fridge for 1 hour.

2. Wash, cut in half and stone the greengages.

3. Roll out the pastry to 4mm and use to line the tart tin (see page 42).

4. Sprinkle 60g of the caster sugar onto the pastry, fill the tart with the halved greengages (cut side up). Brush with a thin layer of egg yolk and sprinkle another 30g of caster sugar over the top.

5. Bake the tart for 40–45 minutes, then cover it up with foil to protect the fruits and finish off the baking for another 20–25 minutes. Remove the foil and cool the tart in the tin.

Sweet shortcrust pastry

How to blind bake a pastry base

1. Line the tart tin with pastry (see page 51) and rest in the fridge for 30 minutes (or place it in the freezer for 10 minutes). Brush the flour off the pastry base using your fingertips or a brush.

2. Cover the pastry base with baking paper or a few layers of heat-resistant cling film and place it gently inside the lined tart tin.

3. Fill the tart case with baking beans or rice/dried beans (I've been using the same short grain rice for years). Blind bake for 35–45 minutes at 160°C/325°F/Gas Mark 3. The thickness of the pastry will determine the baking time.

4. Allow 10 minutes to cool, then remove the baking beans using a large spoon. Remove the baking paper or cling film.

5. Put the tart case back in the oven for an extra 5–10 minutes without the baking beans to even up the colour. The centre of the pastry must be a light golden brown.

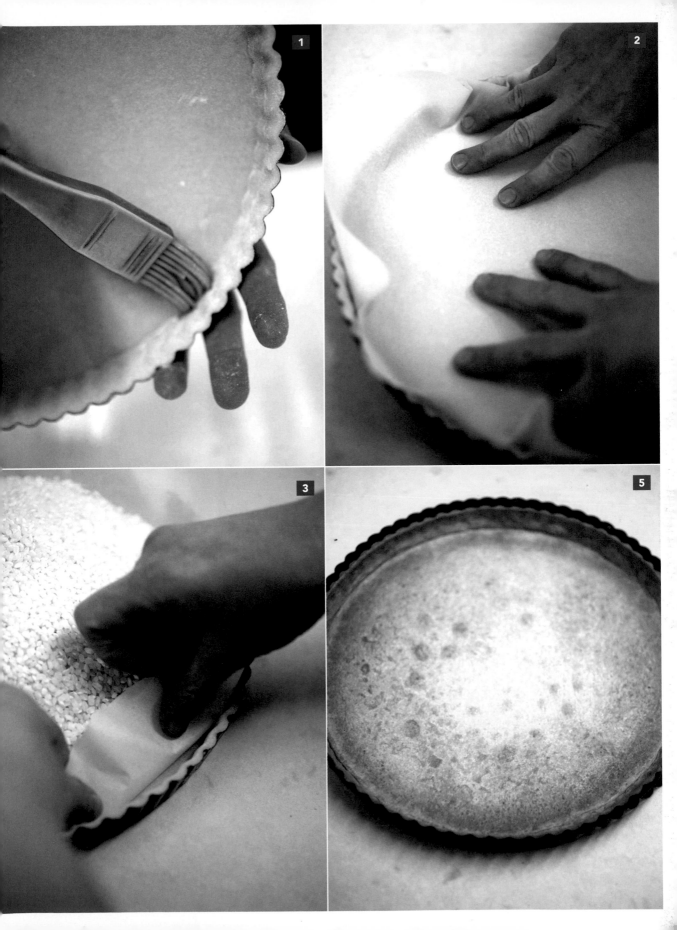

Alsatian apple tart

TARTE ALSACIENNE AUX POMMES

An Alsatian tart is composed of a custard filling and fruits. Any kind of apples can be used for an Alsatian apple tart. Other fruits such as pears, prunes, mirabelles or greengages can also be used.

Serves 10 (24cm high-sided tart) / **Preparation time:** 30 + 20 minutes
Resting time in the fridge: 1 hour + 30 minutes
Baking time: 35–45 + 5–10 + 4 minutes at 160°C/325°F/Gas Mark 3 for the pastry base, 30–40 minutes at 160°C/325°F/Gas Mark 3 with the filling / **You will need a 24cm high-sided tart tin**

INGREDIENTS
500g sweet shortcrust
  pastry (see page 6)
1 beaten egg

For the custard filling
1 egg yolk
2 medium eggs
50g caster sugar
1 vanilla pod (opened
  and scraped) or 1
  teaspoon vanilla
  extract
200ml milk
100ml fresh double
  cream
5 Cox (or Braeburn)
  apples (900g)

1. Make the sweet shortcrust pastry following the method on page 6 and rest in the fridge for 1 hour.

2. Line the tart tin with the pastry (see page 42) and put it in the fridge for 30 minutes.

3. Blind bake the pastry base (see page 50) and leave to cool.

4. Carefully brush the pastry base with the beaten egg. Put it back in the oven for 4 minutes at 160°C/325°F/Gas Mark 3, remove and brush it a second time.

5. To make the filling, whisk together the egg yolk, eggs, caster sugar and vanilla, then add the milk and cream. Pass the mix through a very fine sieve.

6. Peel, cut in half and core the Cox or Braeburn apples. Cut each half into 3 or 4 pieces according to their size. Lay them on the pastry base and pour over the custard to cover $2/3$ of the fruit.

7. Bake the tart until the custard is set and golden brown on top. Cool at room temperature in the tin.

Parisian flan tart

FLAN PARISIEN

This is a classic dessert that you can find in most pâtisserie shops in France. A 'flan' can best be describe as a set custard. Flan powder is traditionally used by pastry chefs and bakers but it's quite hard to find in regular shops. I've replaced it with cornflour here for a very similar result.

Serves 10 (28cm tart) / **Preparation time:** 30 + 15 minutes / **Resting time in the fridge:** 1 hour + 30 minutes / **Baking time:** 35–45 + 5–10 + 4 minutes at 160°C/325°F/Gas Mark 3 for the pastry base, 30–40 minutes at 140°C/275°F/Gas Mark 1 with the filling / **You will need a 28cm tart tin**

INGREDIENTS
500g sweet shortcrust
    pastry (see page 6)
1 beaten egg

For the custard filling
560ml full fat or semi-
    skimmed milk
1 vanilla pod (opened
    and scraped) or 1
    teaspoon of vanilla
    extract
4 medium eggs
75g caster sugar
30g cornflour

1. Make the sweet shortcrust pastry folowing the method on page 6, and rest in the fridge for 1 hour.

2. Line the tart tin (see page 42) with the pastry and put it in the fridge for 30 minutes.

3. Bake blind the pastry base (see page 50) and leave to cool.

4. Carefully brush the pastry base with the beaten egg. Put it back in the oven for 4 minutes at 160°C/325°F/Gas Mark 3, remove and brush it a second time.

5. To make the custard filling, bring the milk and vanilla to the boil. In a large bowl, whisk together the eggs and sugar, then add the cornflour and pour in the boiling milk. Pass the mixture through a very fine sieve.

6. Place the pastry base in the oven and fill to the top with the custard mix using a jug or a ladle. Bake the flan until it is set and golden brown on top. Cool it at room temperature in the tin.

Blueberry and lemon tart

TARTE AUX MYRTILLES CITRONNÉES

Blueberries are common berries in the area in France where I come from. I used to pick them with my sisters when we were little, and my mother would make all sorts of delicious jams, compotes and tarts from them. My blueberry and lemon tart was inspired by these memories.

Serves 10 (28cm tart) / **Preparation time:** 30 + 15 minutes / **Resting time in the fridge:** 1 hour
Baking time: 1 hour at 180°C/350°F/Gas Mark 4 with the fruit filling, 10 minutes at
160°C/325°F/Gas Mark 3 with the lemon cream / **You will need a 28cm tart tin**

INGREDIENTS
500g sweet shortcrust
  pastry (see page 6)
5g baking powder

For the fruit filling
5 punnets of blueberries
  (125g each)
120g caster sugar, to
  taste

For the lemon cream
1 medium egg, separated
25g caster sugar
zest and juice of ¹/₂
  lemon

1. Make the shortcrust pastry following the method on page 6, mixing the baking powder with the flour. Rest in the fridge for 1 hour.

2. Line the tart tin with the pastry (see page 42).

3. Sprinkle 80g caster sugar over the pastry base and cover it with the blueberries and another 40g caster sugar.

4. Bake the tart for 40–45 minutes at 180°C/350°F/Gas Mark 4, then cover it up with foil to protect the fruits and continue to bake for another 15–20 minutes. Remove the tart from the oven and uncover it, then turn the heat down to 160°C/325°F/Gas Mark 3.

5. To make the lemon cream, whisk the egg white to a peak (see page 38) using an electric mixer. In a bowl, whisk the egg yolk with the caster sugar for 2 minutes until it whitens. Fold in the egg white and add the zest and lemon juice.

6. Spread out the lemon cream on top of the blueberry tart and put the tart back in the oven for 10 minutes at 160°C/325°F/Gas Mark 3. Cool in the tin.

✓ CHEF'S TOP TIP

Serve with plain Greek yoghurt, Greek yoghurt ice cream or a spoonful of crème fraîche.

CHAPTER 2

Sweet pastry

LA PÂTE SUCRÉE

Caramelized lemon tart

TARTE CARAMÉLISÉE AU CITRON

This recipe comes from Nico Ladenis' restaurant Chez Nico, and was brought to Historic Sussex Hotels by Martin Hadden when he became executive chef. Over the years, it has become the house dessert at Ockenden Manor, which head chef Stephen Crane and myself are proud to have on the menu.

Serves 12 (24cm high-sided tart) / **Preparation time:** 30 + 20 minutes
Resting time in the fridge: 1 hour + 30 minutes / **Resting time at room temperature:** 4 hours
Baking time: 35–40 + 5–10 minutes at 160°C/325°F/Gas Mark 3 for the pastry base, 40 minutes to
1 hour at 110°C/225°F/Gas Mark ¼ in a static oven (fan off) with the filling
You will need a 24cm high-sided tart tin

INGREDIENTS
500g sweet pastry
   (see page 8)
1 beaten egg

For the lemon cream
9 medium eggs
4 large lemons
250g caster sugar
700g fresh double cream

40g caster sugar to
   caramelize

1. Make the sweet pastry following the method on page 8, and rest in the fridge for 1 hour.

2. Line the tart tin with the pastry (see page 42) and return to the fridge for 30 minutes.

3. Bake blind the pastry base (see page 50) and cool.

4. Carefully brush the pastry base with the beaten egg. Put it back in the oven for 4 minutes at 160°C/325°F/Gas Mark 3, then brush it a second time. Set the base aside, turn the oven temperature down to 110°C/225°F/Gas Mark ¼ and switch off the fan.

5. For the lemon cream, break the eggs into a large bowl and beat them with a whisk. Grate thinly the zest of 3 lemons and mix with the juice of 4 lemons. Put 200g of lemon mix (zest and juice), together with the caster sugar, in a saucepan, and the cream in another. Bring both pans to the boil simultaneously, stirring occasionally. While whisking, pour the boiling lemon mix on top of the beaten egg followed by the boiling cream. Pass the lemon cream through a very fine sieve and skim the surface with a ladle.

6. Fill the tart base evenly with the lemon cream using a small jug and/or a ladle. Place the tart base in the oven (110°C/225°F/Gas Mark ¼, no fan, low shelf). Cook the lemon cream for 40 minutes to 1 hour. Start checking after 35 minutes and then every 5 minutes until it's cooked. The cream should be set like a jelly, gently moving in the middle. Cool at room temperature for a minimum of 4 hours.

7. Cut the lemon tart with a sharp knife. Warm up the blade using a blowtorch or a jug filled with boiling water. Slice the tart and place on

a large tray. Sprinkle some caster sugar on the top of each slice, remove the excess using your index finger and caramelize them with a blowtorch. Serve within 15 minutes with blackcurrent sorbet.

✓ CHEF'S TOP TIP

The white part of the lemon peel is bitter. Grate the surface of the lemon zest carefully to remove only the yellow part.

How to make a
dark chocolate mousse filling

1. Put the chopped chocolate (or chocolate pistoles) and the butter in a bowl.

2. Either melt them in the microwave at a medium power for 1 minute, then check and stir with a spatula. Repeat this step every 30 seconds until both are melted. Or melt them slowly in a heatproof bowl set over a pan of simmering water (a bain-marie, see page 24).

3. Leave to cool for 15 minutes at room temperature.

4. Meanwhile, make a sabayon by whisking together the eggs, egg yolks and caster sugar with an electric mixer for 15 minutes. The sabayon will be 3 times bigger in volume and very light. It must be used straight away.

5. Pour the melted chocolate and butter over the sabayon and combine using a spatula, making a circular movement from the bottom upwards with the spatula in one hand, giving a quarter turn to the bowl with the other.

6. Repeat this step until the chocolate mousse is mixed. Do not overwork it to preserve its lightness. Use straight away to fill the tart or tartlets.

Deliciously light chocolate tart

TARTE AU CHOCOLAT DÉLICIEUSEMENT LÉGÈRE

This tart is a classic dessert of Ockenden Manor. It will make all your thoughts about chocolate desserts being too heavy fly out the window. Enjoy it at room temperature to preserve its lightness and – my advice – hide the rest of it!

Serves 12 (24cm high-sided tart) / **Preparation time:** 30 + 20 minutes / **Resting time in the fridge:** 1 hour + 30 minutes / **Baking time:** 35–45 + 5–10 minutes at 160°C/325°F/Gas Mark 3 for the pastry base. 15 minutes at 120°C/250°F/Gas Mark 1/2 with the chocolate mousse filling
Cooling time at room temperature: 4 hours / **You will need a 24cm high-sided tart tin**

INGREDIENTS
500g sweet pastry
(see page 8)

Dark chocolate mousse filling
340g dark chocolate (55%), chopped
210g butter
4 medium eggs
4 egg yolks
60g caster sugar

1. Make the sweet pastry following the method on page 8, and rest in the fridge for 1 hour.

2. Line the tart tin with the pastry (see page 42) and put it in the fridge for 30 minutes.

3. Bake blind the pastry base for 35–40 minutes (see page 50), then carefully remove the baking beans using a tablespoon and continue baking for about an extra 5–10 minutes until the pastry is evenly golden brown. Turn the oven temperature down to 120°C/250°F/Gas Mark 1/2.

4. While the pastry base is cooling, make the chocolate mousse filling (see page 62).

5. Fill the pastry base with the chocolate mousse and bake it straight away.

6. Leave it to cool at room temperature for a minimum of 4 hours before serving. This chocolate tart can be tricky to cut because the chocolate mousse filling tends to stick to the knife. Warm up the blade of a serrated knife, using a blowtorch or a jug filled with boiling water, and you will get a perfectly clean cut.

👍 GOOD TO KNOW

The percentage of cocoa, in this recipe 55%, represents the quantity of cocoa paste (between 80% and 90%) and cocoa butter in the chocolate. The remaining 45% is mostly composed of sugar. The vanilla aroma and lecithin represent less than 0.5%. The use of a 55% dark chocolate will give the lightness to this mousse. A darker chocolate will set harder at room temperature.

Apricot and almond tart

TARTE AMANDINE AUX ABRICOTS

It's a ritual for me, that each summer, when the apricots are everywhere in the markets and it starts to get warm, I make this tart. There is something delicious about it; almonds and apricots are made for each other.

Serves 10 (28cm tart) / **Preparation time:** 30 + 30 minutes
Resting time in the fridge: 1 hour + 30 minutes / **Baking time:** 35–40 + 5–10 minutes at 160°C/325°F/Gas Mark 3 for the pastry base, 35–45 minutes at 160°C/325°F/Gas Mark 3 with the filling
You will need a 28cm tart tin

INGREDIENTS
500g sweet pastry
  (see page 8)
800g ripe apricots,
  halved
630g almond cream
  (1$^1/_2$ x recipe page 30)

For the apricot jam
  (optional)
250g ripe apricots
80g caster sugar

1. Make the sweet pastry following the method on page 8, and rest in the fridge for 1 hour.

2. For the apricot jam if using, dice the apricots and put them in a pan with the caster sugar. Cook slowly over a low heat for 10 minutes, stirring regularly.

3. Line the tart tin with the pastry (see page 42) and put it in the fridge for 30 minutes.

4. Blind bake the pastry base (see page 50).

5. Make the almond cream following the method on page 30.

5. When the pastry base has cooled, spread over the jam, if using, and cover with the almond cream.

6. Arrange the apricot halves on the top of the tart and bake until evenly golden brown. Cool at room temperature in the tin.

Fig, honey and almond tart

TARTE AMANDINE AU MIEL ET AUX FIGUES

To me, this recipe marks the beginning of autumn. There is something comforting about cooked figs and honey. I recommend you to serve it warm, with yoghurt ice cream and a dash of honey on top.

Serves 10 (28cm tart) / **Preparation time:** 30 + 30 minutes
Resting time in the fridge: 1 hour + 30 minutes / **Baking time:** 35–40 + 5–10 minutes at 160°C/325°F/Gas Mark 3 for the pastry base, 35–45 minutes at 160°C/325°F/Gas Mark 3 with the filling
You will need a 28cm tart tin

INGREDIENTS
500g sweet pastry
  (see page 8)
600g ripe figs, cut into
  quarters

For the fig compote
(optional)
250g ripe figs
50g caster sugar
2 tablespoons water

For the honey and almond
* cream*
165g ground almonds
40g plain flour
165g soft butter, diced
90g caster sugar
75g runny honey
3 medium eggs

For the glaze
20g butter
40g runny honey

1. Make the sweet pastry following the method on page 8, and rest in the fridge for 1 hour.

2. To make the fig compote, if using, cut the figs into small pieces and put them in a pan with the caster sugar and the water. Cook slowly over a low heat for 10 minutes, stirring regularly.

3. Line the tart tin with the pastry (see page 42) and put it in the fridge for 30 minutes.

4. Blind bake the pastry base (see page 50).

5. Make the honey and almond cream following the method on page 30, adding the honey before the eggs.

6. When the pastry base is cold, spread over the fig compote, if using, and cover it evenly with the almond cream.

7. Arrange the quartered figs on top of the tart and bake it until the almond cream is set and golden. Cool it at room temperature in the tin.

8. In a small saucepan, warm up the butter and honey. Glaze the cooled tart with the mixture using a pastry brush.

How to poach pears

1. In a large saucepan, make a syrup by bringing to the boil the water, caster sugar and vanilla pod (opened and scraped).

2. Peel, cut in half and core the pears. Remove the stalks and the fibre around the core. If the pears are not to be used straight away, sprinkle them with the juice of half a lemon.

3. Cut a sheet of baking paper 2cm wider than the rim of the saucepan.

4. When the syrup is boiling, turn the heat down and put the halved pears inside the pan one at a time.

5. Cover the pears with the baking paper and put a plate or something similar on top of it (I used the loose bottom of a cake tin). This will stop the pears from floating and allow them to cook evenly without browning. The fruits must be immersed in the syrup during cooking.

6. Turn the heat up. The syrup must be simmering but not boiling and the cooking time depends on the ripeness of the fruits. After 20 minutes, prick the pears with a wooden cocktail stick or a small knife. It must penetrate the fruit easily. Continue to simmer, checking every 5 minutes, until cooked.

7. When the pears are cooked, remove the pan from the heat and cool at room temperature. The fruits must still be immersed in the syrup while cooling down.

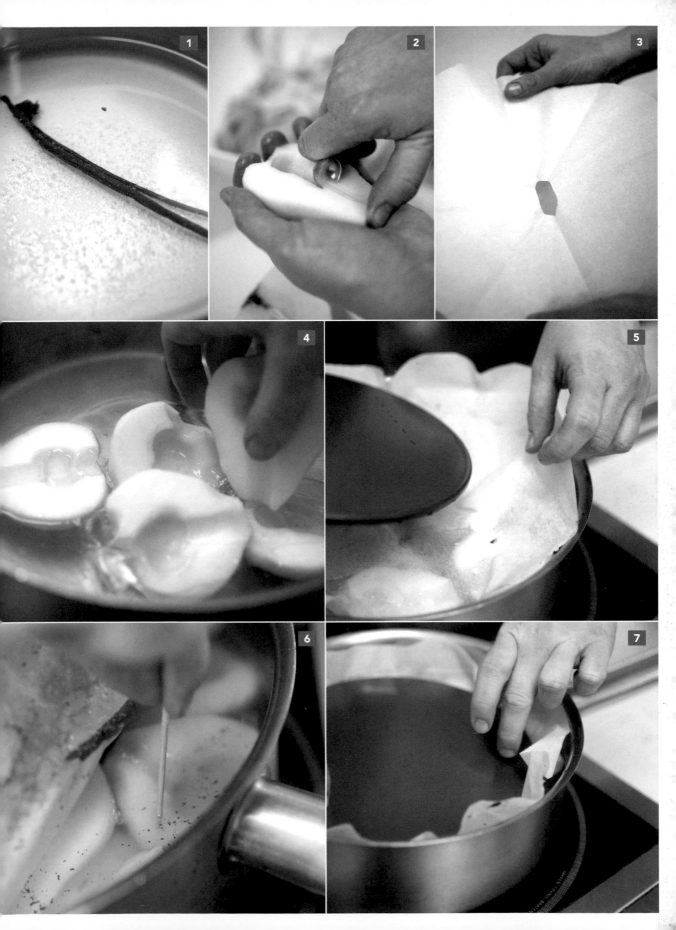

Pear, chocolate and almond tart

TARTE AMANDINE AU CHOCOLAT ET AUX POIRES

This is my French version of a pear Bakewell tart. I always loved the combination of pear and chocolate, and with the almonds it becomes just magical.

Serves 8 (24cm tart) / **Preparation time:** 30 + 30 minutes
Resting time in the fridge: 1 hour + 30 minutes / **Baking time:** 35–40 + 5–10 minutes at 160°C/325°F/Gas Mark 3 for the pastry base, 35–45 minutes at 160°C/325°F/Gas Mark 3 with the filling
You will need a 12x35cm rectangular tart tin or a 24cm round tart tin

INGREDIENTS

For the poached pears
5 Williams pears
1 litre water
300g caster sugar
1 vanilla pod (opened
  and scraped)

For the cocoa sweet pastry
20g cocoa powder
170g plain flour
1 small pinch of salt
140g cold butter, diced
1 medium egg
55g caster sugar

*For the chocolate and
  almond cream*
135g ground almonds
35g plain flour
85g soft butter, diced
165g sugar
3 medium eggs
85g dark chocolate
  (70%), chopped
80g butter

1. Prepare and poach the pears (see page 70). This step can be done the day before.

2. Sift the cocoa powder with the flour and make the sweet pastry following the method on page 8. Rest in the fridge for 1 hour.

3. Line the tart tin with the pastry (see page 42) and return it to the fridge for 30 minutes.

4. Blind bake the pastry base (see page 50).

5. For the chocolate and almond cream, make an almond cream following the method on page 30. Melt the chocolate and 80g of butter in the microwave at a medium power, stirring every 30 seconds until it's melted, then incorporate it into the almond cream using a spatula.

6. When the pastry base has cooled, spread evenly with the chocolate almond cream.

7. Garnish the tart with the poached pear halves and bake it until the chocolate almond cream is set and cooked. Cool at room temperature in the tin.

Basque custard and black cherry pie

GÂTEAU BASQUE

I discovered this pie when I was a teenager during a family summer holiday in the French Basque country. Back home when I made it with my mother for the first time, it was a real success!

Serves 10 (24cm pie) / **Preparation time:** 1 hour
Resting time in the fridge: 2 + 1 hours / **Baking time:** 40–50 minutes at 180°C/350°F/Gas Mark 4
You will need a 24cm round cake tin

INGREDIENTS
450g crème pâtissière
   (see page 28)

For the pastry
150g caster sugar
1 medium egg
1 egg yolk
zest of 1/2 lemon, thinly
   grated
1/2 teaspoon salt
150g plain flour
200g soft butter

For the black cherry jam
   (or use a small jar of
   black cherry jam)
250g black cherries
110g caster sugar

For the glaze
1 egg yolk
1 teaspoon water

✓ CHEF'S TOP TIP
   A raspberry
   compote or jam also
   makes a delicious
   filling instead of the
   black cherry jam.

1. Make the crème pâtissière following the method and recipe on page 28.

2. To make the pastry, use an electric mixer to whisk the caster sugar, egg, egg yolk, thinly grated lemon zest and salt until it whitens. Switch the whisk to the paddle attachment and mix in the flour followed by the soft butter. Divide the pastry into 2 unequal pieces (250g for the top, 330g for the base), cover in cling film and rest in the fridge for 1 hour.

3. To make the black cherry jam; stone and cut the cherries into quarters. Put them in a pan with the caster sugar, and cook the jam slowly over a low heat for about 10 minutes to reduce the juice. Cool at room temperature.

4. Remove the larger piece of pastry from the fridge and use to line the tart tin (see page 42)

5. Spread the cherry jam evenly over the pastry, then cover it with the whisked crème pâtissière.

6. Brush the side of the pastry base with water. Roll out the second pastry section and cover the pie. Remove the excess and seal the lid to the base by pinching the pastry edges together.

7. With a pastry brush, mix the egg yolk with the water and glaze the pie. Mark some ridges with a fork and make a hole in its middle with a knife tip.

8. Bake the pie for 30 minutes. If the top gets too dark, cover it with a piece of foil before finishing off the baking. Cool down in the dish.

Walnut tart

TARTE AUX NOIX

This is quite an unusual tart but should definitively be tasted. I recommend you try it with coffee ice cream or serve it with coffee.

Serves 8 (for a 24cm tart) / **Preparation time:** 30 + 20 minutes
Resting time in the fridge: 1 hour + 30 minutes / **Baking time:** 35–40 + 5–10 minutes at 160°C/325°F/Gas Mark 3 for the pastry base, 30–40 minutes at 160°C/325°F/Gas Mark 3 with the filling
You will need a 24cm tart tin

INGREDIENTS
500g sweet pastry (see page 8)

For the walnut cream
150g butter
250g caster sugar
250g broken walnuts
3 medium eggs

1. Make the sweet pastry following the method on page 8, and rest in the fridge for 1 hour.

2. Line the tart tin with the pastry (see page 42) and put it in the fridge for 30 minutes.

3. Blind bake the pastry base (see page 50).

4. Make the walnut cream. Using an electric mixer fitted with a paddle, cream the butter and sugar, then alternately add batches of the broken walnuts and the eggs.

5. When the pastry base has cooled, spread out the walnut cream evenly then bake the tart until the cream is set and golden brown. Cool at room temperature in the tin.

CHAPTER 3

Sablée pastry

LA PÂTE SABLÉE

Sour cherry and pistachio tartlets

TARTELETTES À LA PISTACHE ET AUX CERISES GRIOTTES

The acidity of the sour cherry contrasts marvellously with the sweetness of the pistachio cream. It's a perfect balance of flavour, combined in a colourful and pretty tartlet.

Makes 10 / **Preparation time:** 30 + 20 minutes / **Resting time in the fridge:** 1 hour
Resting time in the freezer: 15 minutes / **Baking time:** 10–12 minutes at 160°C/325°F/Gas Mark 3
for the tartlet bases, 15–20 minutes at 160°C/325°F/Gas Mark 3 with the filling
You will need 10 x 10cm tartlet moulds

INGREDIENTS
500g sablée pastry
  (see page 10)

For the pistachio cream
90g ground pistachios
  (or whole and ground
  in a food processor)
25g plain flour
110g soft butter, diced
110g caster sugar
2 medium eggs

For the cherry jam
  (or use a jar of cherry
  jam)
100g red or black
  cherries, stoned
50g caster sugar (or 75g
  for red cherry jam)

For the cherry topping
200g stoned red morello
  cherries (fresh, frozen
  or from a jar)

1. Make the sablée pastry following the method on page 12, and rest in the fridge for 1 hour.

2. Line the tartlet tins with the pastry (see page 42), prick several times with a fork and put them in the freezer for 15 minutes.

3. Make the pistachio cream following the method on page 202 (same method as almond cream) and keep it at room temperature.

4. For the cherry jam, put the cherries in a pan with the caster sugar. Cook slowly over a low heat for 10 minutes, stirring regularly.

5. Put the tartlet bases on a baking tray. Bake blind straight from the freezer without baking beans. After 8 minutes of baking, turn the tray in the oven and bake for another 2–4 minutes. The tartlets must be evenly golden brown but not too dark. Leave to cool.

6. When the tartlet bases are cold, add 1 teaspoon of cherry jam to each, cover with 1 tablespoon of pistachio cream and push in 8–10 stoned morello cherries. Bake until the pistachio cream is set and golden. Remove from the tins and cool on a wire rack.

How to make a white chocolate and vanilla mousse

1. Soften the gelatine leaves in cold water for 10 minutes.

2. Break the white chocolate into small pieces and put it in a large bowl.

3. Drain off the water from the gelatine leaves and add them to the white chocolate.

4. Bring to the boil the fresh double cream with the vanilla pod (opened and scraped), and pour it over the white chocolate through a fine sieve.

5. Stir with a spatula until the chocolate is melted, then cool for 15 minutes at room temperature.

6. Fold in the softly whipped cream.

7. Set in the fridge for a minimum of 4 hours before use.

Raspberry and white chocolate tart

TARTE AUX FRAMBOISES ET AU CHOCOLAT BLANC VANILLÉ

If I had to pick a favourite tart, this would probably be it. Personally, it's the perfect combination of flavours and textures: a crispy nutty pastry, a sweet chocolate cream that contrasts with the acidity of the fresh raspberries. Just divine!

Serves 8 (24cm tart) / **Preparation time:** 30 + 20 minutes / **Resting time in the fridge:** 4 + 1 hours + 15 minutes / **Resting time in the freezer:** 15 minutes / **Baking time:** 15–20 minutes at 160°C/325°F/Gas Mark 3 / **You will need a 24cm tart tin**

INGREDIENTS

For the white chocolate and vanilla mousse
2 small gelatine leaves (3g)
120g white chocolate
200mlg fresh double cream
1 vanilla pod (opened and scraped)
280ml fresh double cream, softly whipped

For the hazelnut sablée pastry
80g ground hazelnuts
180g plain flour
120g cold butter, diced
120g icing sugar
small pinch of salt
1 medium egg

For the filling
100g white chocolate
20g butter
600g fresh raspberries (about 6 punnets)
150g raspberry jam
1 tablespoon water

1. Make the white chocolate and vanilla mousse (see page 82). Set in the fridge for a minimum of 4 hours. This step can be done the day before.

2. Mix the ground hazelnuts with the flour and make the sablée pastry following the method on page 10. Rest in the fridge for 1 hour.

3. Line the tart tin (see page 42), prick with a fork and put it in the freezer for 15 minutes.

4. Blind bake the pastry base straight from the freezer (no baking beans needed) until it is evenly golden brown.

5. Melt the white chocolate and butter together in the microwave at a medium power for 1 minute. Stir with a spatula and repeat this step every 30 seconds until the chocolate is completely melted. Brush the pastry base with a thin layer of the chocolate and butter mix. Set in the fridge for 15 minutes. This will help the pastry to stay crispy.

6. Fill a piping bag and pipe a thin layer of the white chocolate mousse over the chocolate-coated pastry. Top the tart with the raspberries.

7. In a pan, warm up the raspberry jam with the water and use to glaze the raspberries using a pastry brush.

Strawberry tart

This is the one dessert that we all love to see in pastry-shop windows. It's so pretty and fresh that we devour it with our eyes. Try it at home – it's sure to be a success.

Serves 8 (24cm tart) / **Preparation time:** 1 hour / **Resting time in the fridge:** 2 + 1 hours
Resting time in the freezer: 15 minutes / **Baking time:** 15–20 minutes at 160°C/325°F/Gas Mark 3
You will need a 24cm tart tin

INGREDIENTS
450g crème pâtissière
   (see page 28)

*For the almond sablée
   pastry*
80g ground almonds
180g plain flour
small pinck of salt
120g icing sugar
120g cold butter, diced
1 medium egg

For the filling
100g white chocolate
20g butter
600g small strawberries
   (2–3 punnets)

For the glaze
150g strawberry jam
1 tablespoon water

1. Make the crème pâtissière following the method on page 28, and rest in the fridge for 2 hours.

2. Add the ground almonds to the flour and make the sablée pastry according to the method on page 10. Rest in the fridge for 1 hour.

3. Line the tart tin with the pastry (see page 42), prick with a fork and put it in the freezer for 15 minutes.

4. Put the tart on a baking tray and bake blind straight out of the freezer without baking beans. After 15 minutes of baking, turn the tray in the oven and bake for another 2–5 minutes. The tart should be golden brown all over but not too dark.

5. Melt the white chocolate and butter in the microwave at a medium power for 1 minute. Stir with a spatula and repeat this step every 30 seconds until the chocolate is completely melted. Brush the pastry base with a thin layer of the chocolate mix. Set in the fridge for 15 minutes. This will help the pastry to stay crispy.

6. Put the strawberries in a colander and wash them quickly under cold water. Drain and put them on a kitchen cloth to dry. Remove the hulls and cut in half.

7. Fill a piping bag with the crème pâtissière without working it, and pipe it onto the pastry base. Flatten it out with the back of a tablespoon and garnish the tart with the strawberry halves.

8. In a pan, slowly warm up the strawberry jam and the water. Use to glaze the tart using a pastry brush.

GOOD TO KNOW
   If you don't have a piping bag you can use a freezer bag with the

corner snipped off to pipe the crème pâtissière. This tart is quite fragile and shouldn't be put together too far in advance. I would recommend making it no more than 4 hours before serving (and eat within 24 hours). Keep it in the fridge and take it out 30 minutes before eating.

Warm chocolate tartlets

This is the perfect dessert to finish an elegant meal at home with friends. The tartlets can be made in advance and then cooked and served straight away at dessert time. Their hot and runny chocolate centres will amaze your guests.

Makes 8 / **Preparation time:** 30 + 20 minutes / **Resting time in the fridge:** 1 hour
Resting time in the freezer: 15 minutes / **Baking time:** 10–12 minutes at 160°C/325°F/Gas Mark 3
for the tartlet bases, 7–10 minutes at 180°C/350°F/Gas Mark 4 with the filling
You will need 8 x 10cm tartlet tins

INGREDIENTS

8 dark chocolate squares
(55%)

*For the chocolate sablée
  pastry*
20g cocoa powder
240g plain flour
120g cold butter, diced
120g icing sugar
small pinch of salt
1 medium egg

*For the chocolate mousse
  filling*
105g butter
170g dark chocolate
(55%)
2 medium eggs
2 egg yolks
30g caster sugar

1. Mix the cocoa powder with the flour and make the sablée pastry following the method on page 10. Rest in the fridge for 1 hour.

2. Line the tartlet tins with the pastry (see page 42), prick with a fork and put them in the freezer for 15 minutes.

3. Put the tartlets on a baking tray and bake them blind straight from the freezer without baking beans. After 8 minutes of baking, turn the tray in the oven and bake for another 2–4 minutes. The tartlets should be evenly golden brown but not too dark.

4. Cool the tartlets on a tray, in their tins, and place a chocolate square in each one.

5. Make the chocolate mousse filling following the method on page 60, and fill the tartlet bases to the top using a tablespoon or a piping bag. Set in the fridge.

6. Bake the tartlets. Check after 7 minutes, turn the tray in the oven then keep checking them minute by minute. The chocolate tartlets have to be baked, removed from their tins and served straight away. Take them out of the oven when their centres still look wet; the centres should be runny when you break them with a spoon.

Lemon meringue pies

TARTELETTES MERINGUÉES AU CITRON

This is the French version of the caramelized lemon tart on page 60: a crunchy pastry and a sweet meringue on top of a sharp lemon cream. This combination of taste and texture brings a little 'je ne sais quoi' to the pies that I find really enjoyable.

Makes 8 / **Preparation time:** 30 + 20 minutes / **Resting time in the fridge:** 1 hour
Resting time in the freezer: 15 minutes / **Baking time:** 10–12 minutes at 160°C/325°F/Gas Mark 3
You will need 8 x 10cm tartlet tins

INGREDIENTS
500g sablée pastry
  (see page 10)

For the lemon cream
150ml lemon juice
4 egg yolks
2 medium eggs
105g caster sugar
105g soft butter

For the French meringue
3 egg whites (120g)
200g caster sugar

1. Make the sablée pastry following the method on page 10, and rest in the fridge for 1 hour.

2. To make the lemon cream, put the lemon juice, egg yolks, eggs and caster sugar in a saucepan. Bring it to the boil, stirring continuously with a whisk. Pass the mixture through a very fine sieve and leave it to cool to 30°C at room temperature. Incorporate the soft butter using a hand mixer, then set in the fridge.

3. Line the tartlet tins with the pastry, prick with a fork and put them in the freezer for 15 minutes.

4. Place the tartlets on a baking tray and bake them blind straight from the freezer without baking beans. After 8 minutes of baking, turn the tray in the oven and bake for another 2–4 minutes. The tartlets should be evenly golden brown but not too dark.

5. Remove the cold tartlets from their tins and fill them with the lemon cream.

6. Make the French meringue following the method on page 36. Fill a piping bag fitted with a fluted nozzle with the mixture and decorate the tartlets.

7. Blowtorch the meringue by placing the flame close to it and moving the flame quickly across the meringue, or bake the pies cold from the fridge for 2 minutes at 240°C/475°F/Gas Mark 9.

Milk chocolate and hazelnut tartlets

TARTELETTES À LA NOISETTE ET AU CHOCOLAT AU LAIT

Rich in milk chocolate, these tartlets are a perfect match for summer berries. You could also serve them with a scoop of a good-quality passion fruit sorbet if you want to surprise your guests with an original combination worthy of a Michelin-starred restaurant.

Makes 10 / **Preparation time:** 30 + 30 minutes / **Resting time in the fridge:** 1 + 1 hour
Resting time in the freezer: 15 minutes / **Baking time:** 10–12 minutes at 160°C/325°F/Gas Mark 3
You will need 10 x 10cm tartlet tins

INGREDIENTS

For the hazelnut sablée pastry
80g ground hazelnuts
180g plain flour
120g cold butter, diced
120g icing sugar
½ teaspoon salt
1 medium egg

For the milk chocolate filling
200g crème anglaise (see page 26)
200g milk chocolate
100ml fresh double cream

For the marinated berries
100g strawberries, hulled and quartered
100g raspberries
50g blueberries
10g caster sugar

1. Mix the ground hazelnuts with the flour and make the sablée pastry following the method on page 10. Rest in the fridge for 1 hour.

2. Line the tartlet tins with the pastry (see page 42), prick with a fork and put in the freezer for 15 minutes.

3. Place the tartlets on a baking tray and blind bake them straight from the freezer without baking beans. After 8 minutes of baking, turn the tray in the oven and bake for another 2–4 minutes. The tartlets should be evenly golden brown but not too dark.

4. Make the crème anglaise following the method on page 26, and weigh out 200g.

5. Melt the milk chocolate in the microwave at medium power for 1 minute. Stir with a spatula and repeat this step every 30 seconds until the chocolate is melted.

6. For the milk chocolate filling, pour the hot crème anglaise on top of the melted milk chocolate in 4 batches, stirring each time with a spatula. Whisk the cream until it is softly whipped and fold it into the chocolate mix. Fill the tartlets to the top and set in the fridge for 1 hour.

7. To marinate the berries, half an hour before serving, put the strawberries, raspberries and blueberries in a bowl and sprinkle with caster sugar. Keep at room temperature and stir occasionally. Serve with the tartlets and/or use to decorate.

CHAPTER 4

Puff pastry

LA PÂTE FEUILLETÉE

Apple tart Tatin

TARTE TATIN AUX POMMES

Created in the nineteenth-century in the restaurant of the Tatin sisters at Lamotte-Beuvron in the centre of France, legend has it that the tart was born from a mistake. A burnt apple tart was saved by keeping the caramelized apples and baking them with a pastry top. The cooked pie was then turned out and served upside down.

Serves 10 (24cm tart) / **Preparation time:** 40 minutes + 1 hour / **Resting time in the fridge:** 2¹/₂ hours
Baking time: 30–40 minutes at 200°C/400°F/Gas Mark 6
You will need a 24cm heavy-based ovenproof tart tin

INGREDIENTS
400g puff pastry
 (see page 12)

For the apple topping
15 small Cox or
 Braeburn apples
200g caster sugar
75g butter

1. Make the puff pastry following the method on page 12. This step can be done the day before.

2. Peel, cut in half and core the apples.

3. In a heavy-based ovenproof dish that you can also use on the hob, or an ovenproof frying pan, make a soft caramel by melting together the butter and caster sugar on a medium heat until the liquid is golden brown but not too dark.

4. Off the heat, tightly pack the apple halves into the dish and cook them slowly on the stove for 20–30 minutes with a lid on. The soft caramel will start to cook and colour the apples from the bottom to the top. Remove from the heat and leave to cool for 30 minutes in the dish.

5. Roll out the puff pastry (2.5–3mm thickness) and cut a round base 1.5cm wider than the tart dish. Prick it with a fork on both sides.

6. Cover the apples with the pastry. Fold in the excess pastry, pushing down and tucking in the edges all around the inside between the dish and the fruit. With a knife tip, make a few holes in the pastry to allow the steam to escape.

7. Bake the tart Tatin until the puff pastry is golden brown, then cool it in the dish. Before serving, flash the tart in the oven for 5 minutes at 200°C/400°F/Gas Mark 6 and then turn it over carefully onto a tray.

👍 GOOD TO KNOW

A pear tart Tatin can also be made following the same method and using Williams pears, but make sure they're not too ripe. If you're short on time, you can use a shortcrust pastry (see page 6) instead of the puff pastry, which is just what my mother would do.

Summer fruits puff tartlets

TARTELETTES FEUILLETÉES AUX FRUITS D'ÉTÉ

I just love these tartlets; they remind me of my childhood when my sister Isabelle and I used to stop at the pâtisserie on our way home from school. They looked so pretty, and even now it's still very hard to decide which one to pick!

**Makes 8 / Preparation time: 40 + 50 minutes / Resting time in the fridge: 2¹/₂ hours
Baking time: 15–20 minutes at 200°C/400°F/Gas Mark 6
You will need a non-stick baking tray**

INGREDIENTS
500g puff pastry
  (see page 12)
225g crème pâtissière
  (¹/₂ recipe on page 28)
1 beaten egg

For the fruit garnish
100g strawberries
100g raspberries
100g blueberries
(Or 300g any fruits of
  your choice)

For the glaze
150g raspberry jam
1 tablespoon water

1. Make the puff pastry following the method on page 12. This step can be done the day before.

2. Make a crème pâtissière (see page 28) and rest in the fridge for 2 hours.

3. Roll out the puff pastry to a 40 x 30cm rectangle, 3mm thick. Remove the excess flour on the top and underneath it. Trim the edges with a knife in order to get a perfect rectangular shape.

4. With a large knife, cut in from the long side 4 bands 2cm wide. Divide the rest into 2 bands, 16cm wide.

5. Prick with a fork the 2 widest bands of pastry on both sides. Brush both sides of each band with egg and place the 4 smallest bands of pastry on top of them. Press gently with the fingertips to seal and mark the side with a knife tip. Brush the sides with the beaten egg. Lay the pastry bases on a non-stick baking tray and rest for 30 minutes in the fridge before baking until golden brown. Cool on wire rack.

6. Fill a piping bag with the crème pâtissière without working it and pipe a thin layer onto each band of cooked puff pastry. A tablespoon can also be used (but in this case, the crème pâtissière must be whisked before use in order to soften it).

7. Divide each band into 4 individual tartlets using a serrated knife. Garnish with the fruits of your choice.

8. In a pan over a low heat, warm up the raspberry jam and the water. Use to glaze the tartlets with a pastry brush.

Fine plum tart

In France, a classic fine tart would be made with apples. But the chef in me decided otherwise when I saw some amazing plums in the market one day. I made a fine plum tart for the first time and it was so good that the recipe had to be in this book.

Serves 8 / **Preparation time:** 40 + 30 minutes / **Resting time in the fridge:** 2¹/₂ hours / **Resting time in the freezer:** 30 minutes / **Baking time:** 10 minutes at 210°C/425°F/Gas Mark 7 + 25–30 minutes at 180°C/350°F/Gas Mark 4 / **You will need a non-stick baking tray**

INGREDIENTS
500g puff pastry
  (see page 12)
1 beaten egg

For the plum compote
4 ripe red plums, diced
80–100g caster sugar, to
  taste

For the garnish
10 red plums (700-
  800g)
40g caster sugar

1. Make the puff pastry following the method on page 12. This step can be done the day before.

2. For the plum compote, put the diced plums and caster sugar in a pan and cook over a low heat for 15 minutes, stirring regularly.

3. Roll out the puff pastry to a 30 x 30cm square, 3mm thick. Remove the excess flour on the top and underneath it. Trim the edges with a knife in order to get a perfect square shape.

4. With a large knife, cut a 25cm square from the puff pastry. Use the trimmings to cut 4 bands (25 x 2cm) for the crust. Cut each end of the band at a 45-degree angle to fit the pastry base.

5. Prick the pastry base with a fork, turn it over onto a baking tray and prick it again. Brush the sides of the pastry base with egg and lay on top the 4 bands for the crust. Press firmly with your fingertips to seal. Brush with egg and decorate the sides with the tip of a knife.

6. Spread the plum compote inside the pastry base.

7. Cut in half and stone the plums. Slice them and use to garnish the tart. Sprinkle the caster sugar on the fruit and brush the crust with egg. Put the tart in the freezer for 30 minutes before baking until the pastry base is evenly golden brown underneath. Use a spatula to lift up the tart and check its colour. Cool on a wire rack.

👍 GOOD TO KNOW

Cooking at a high temperature helps the puff pastry to develop and rise in the oven. But in order for the pastry to cook evenly, especially the part underneath the fruit or cream, the oven temperature must be turned down to finish off the baking. Otherwise the crust around the tart will become too dark, too quickly, while the pastry underneath will not have enough time to cook.

Twelfth Night cake: almond pithivier

GALETTE DES ROIS

This cake is eaten in France on Twelfth Night. The tradition is that a child will hide under the table and assign a slice of cake to each guest. The one who finds the hidden charm in the cake will become the king or queen and will be crowned with a paper crown. This person will then get to choose their king or a queen and give that person the second paper crown.

Serves 10 (25cm cake) / **Preparation time:** 40 + 45 minutes / **Resting time in the fridge:** 2^1/$_2$ hours
Resting time in freezer: 30 minutes / **Baking time:** 10 minutes at 220°C/425°F/Gas Mark 7 + 25–35 minutes at 180°C/350°F/Gas Mark 4 / **You will need a non-stick baking tray**

INGREDIENTS
800g puff pastry
  (see page 12)
A charm to hide in the
  cake
1 beaten egg, to glaze

For the frangipane cream
110g crème pâtissière
  (^{1}/$_4$ recipe see page 28)
420g almond cream
  (see page 30)

For the syrup
50g caster sugar
25ml water

1. Make the puff pastry following the method on page 12.

2. Make a crème pâtissière following the method on page 28 and rest in the fridge for 2 hours.

3. Make the almond cream (see page 30) and keep it at room temperature.

4. In a large bowl, whisk 110g of crème pâtissière and fold in the almond cream in 3 or 4 additions. Set aside at room temperature.

5. Divide the puff pastry into 2 unequal pieces (about 350g and 450g). Roll out the smallest piece to 3mm thick and cut a round pastry base about 28cm in diameter. Brush the flour off and place it on a non-stick baking tray or a tray lined with baking paper.

6. Put the frangipane cream in its middle, leaving a 4cm gap from the edge of the pastry, and put the charm in the cream away from the centre. Brush the sides of the pastry base with egg.

7. Roll out the largest piece of puff pastry to 3mm thick, brush the flour off and put it over the frangipane cream and pastry base. Press firmly with the fingertips to seal the sides. With a knife, remove the excess pastry, leaving a 3–4cm gap between the cream and the edge of the puff pastry, then brush the cake with beaten egg. With a knife tip, make a hole in the centre to allow the steam to escape and draw a rosette. Glaze a second time and rest in the freezer for 30 minutes before baking until the bottom of the cake is evenly golden brown.

8. To make the syrup, put the caster sugar and water in a pan and bring to the boil. About 5 minutes before the end of baking, remove the cake from the oven and brush it with syrup. Finish baking, then cool on a wire rack and serve warm.

Cherry and hazelnut pithiviers

PITHIVIERS À LA NOISETTE ET AUX CERISES

This is my grown-up version of the classic Twelfth Night cake. I recommend you serve it warm with the red wine and cherry compote.

Makes 8 / **Preparation time:** 40 + 40 minutes / **Resting time in the fridge:** 2½ hours + 15 minutes
Resting time in freezer: 30 minutes / **Baking time:** 20-25 minutes at 200°C/400°F/Gas Mark 6
You will need a non-stick baking tray and 2 pastry cutters (90 and 100mm) or similar (glasses, bowls or mugs turned upside down and a knife to cut)

INGREDIENTS
500g puff pastry
  (see page 12)
1 beaten egg, to glaze

For the filling
210g hazelnut cream
  (½ almond recipe, on
  page 30)
24–32 stoned cherries
  cut into halves

For the syrup
50g caster sugar
25ml water

1. Make the puff pastry following the method on page 12.

2. Make the hazelnut cream (see page 30), using ground hazelnuts instead of ground almonds. Set aside at room temperature.

3. Roll out the puff pastry to 3mm thick and remove the excess flour on both sides. With 2 pastry cutters (90 and 100mm), cut 8 pithiviers bases and 8 tops. Rest them in the fridge for 15 minutes.

4. Remove the 8 pithivier bases (the smaller ones) from the fridge and brush with beaten egg. Put a large teaspoon of hazelnut cream in their centres and 6–8 cherry halves. Leave 2cm gaps to seal the tops.

5. Remove the 8 tops from the fridge and place one over each pithivier. Press firmly around the sides with your fingertips to seal.

6. Remove the excess pastry using a knife or a pastry cutter, leaving a 2cm gap between the cream and the edge of the pastry. Brush the top of the pithiviers with beaten egg. With a knife tip, make a hole in their centres to allow the steam to escape and draw on a pattern. Glaze once more and leave for 30 minutes in the freezer before baking.

7. For the syrup, put the caster sugar and the water in a pan and bring to the boil. About 5 minutes before the end of baking, remove the pithiviers from the oven and brush them with syrup. Finish baking and cool on a wire rack. Serve warm.

Apple and blackberry turnovers

CHAUSSONS AUX POMMES ET À LA MÛRE

This recipe is the perfect illustration of how living in England influenced my baking. I have changed the classic French apple turnover into an apple and blackberry one. And it's oh-so good!

Makes 8 / **Preparation time:** 40 + 30 minutes / **Resting time in the fridge:** 2¹⁄₂ hours
Resting time in freezer: 1 hour / **Baking time:** 20-25 minutes at 200°C/400°F/Gas Mark 6
You will need a non-stick baking tray

INGREDIENTS
500g puff pastry
  (see page 12)
1 beaten egg, to glaze

*For the apple and
  blackberry compote*
2 small Bramley apples,
  peeled, cored and
  diced
150g blackberries
20g butter
120–150g caster sugar,
  to taste
1 tablespoon water

1. Make the puff pastry following the method on page 12. This step can be done the day before.

2. To make the compote, put the diced apples, blackberries, butter, caster sugar and water in a pan and cook them slowly over a low heat for 15 minutes. Stir regularly. Cool the compote at room temperature.

3. Roll out the puff pastry to 4mm thick and remove the excess flour on both sides. Cut 8 circles of 15cm using a bowl turned upside down and a knife, and roll them into oval shapes with a rolling pin.

4. Put 2 small tablespoons of compote just underneath the centre of each circle and spread out in a half-circle leaving 3cm around the edge free from compote to seal the pastry. Brush the sides with egg and fold the puff pastry in half. With your fingertips, press firmly on the sides to seal the pastry.

5. With a small knife, trim off the excess pastry and shape the turnovers into half-circles leaving a large band of puff pastry around the compote. Place them on a non-stick baking tray and brush with beaten egg. Make some drawings with a knife tip without cutting through the pastry and glaze them a second time. Make a hole in its centre and rest in the freezer for 1 hour before baking. Cool on a wire rack.

👍 GOOD TO KNOW
The resting time in the freezer is optional, but I always do it. Using frozen compote makes it less likely the turnovers will leak during baking.

Vanilla millefeuille

MILLE-FEUILLE À LA VANILLE

A true classic beauty! This slice is so elegant that you never quite know how to eat it without destroying all the layers. A sharp serrated knife can be a solution but it's more fun just to dig in.

Serves 10 (1 large millefeuille) / **Preparation time:** 40 + 45 minutes
Resting time in the fridge: 2 hours + 45 minutes /
Baking time: 25–30 minutes at 180°C/350°F/Gas Mark 4 / **You will need 2 baking trays**

INGREDIENTS
800g puff pastry
  (see page 12)
900g crème pâtissière
  (2 x recipe page 28)
200g diced almonds
40g dark chocolate

For the glaze
250g white fondant
(Or 250g white icing +
  30–40ml boiling
  water)

1. Make the puff pastry following the method on page 12. This step can be done the day before.

2. Make the crème pâtissière (see page 28) and rest in the fridge for a minimum of 2 hours. This step can also be done the day before.

3. Divide the puff pastry into 3 equal pieces. Roll each out to a 4mm-thick square. Remove any excess flour and prick them on both sides with a fork. Put the squares on baking trays and rest them in the fridge for 30 minutes before baking to prevent them from shrinking.

4. Place each sheet of puff pastry between 2 sheets of baking paper, then between 2 baking trays, to stop them from rising excessively. Bake for 20 minutes, then remove the trays from the oven and press on them using your body weight to flatten them out. Check the colour of the puff pastry, turn the trays and put them back in the oven to finish baking for 5–10 minutes; it should be evenly golden brown. Cool on a wire rack.

5. Toast the diced almonds in the oven for 10 minutes at 150°C/300°F/Gas Mark 2. Stir after 5 minutes.

6. Trim the puff-pastry sheets, one at a time, into 3 squares of 20cm. Fill a piping bag fitted with a medium-size nozzle with the set crème pâtissière.

7. Assemble the millefeuille: put the first square of puff pastry on a tray, pipe over evenly the crème pâtissière to cover it and put the second square of pastry on top. Pipe another layer of crème pâtissière and lay on the final square of pastry. Put in the fridge for 15 minutes.

8. Melt the chocolate in the microwave (or in a bain-marie, see page 24) at medium power for 1 minute, then check and stir with a spatula. Repeat this step every 30 seconds until the chocolate is melted. Make a paper cone from baking paper, fill it with the chocolate and keep warm.

9. In a pan or in the microwave, slowly warm up the white fondant to 36–37°C. Alternatively, put the white icing in a bowl and warm it (35–40°C) in the microwave at medium power. Put it in the bowl of an electric mixer fitted with a paddle, work the white icing and hot water until the mix softens and becomes runny.

10. To finish off the millefeuille, spread over the glaze while it is still warm and pipe on some straight lines with the chocolate. Marble the glaze using the tip of a knife in a criss-cross pattern.

11. Spread some crème patisserie over the sides and coat with the toasted diced almonds.

✓ CHEF'S ADVICE
The puff pastry will absorb the moisture of the cream rather quickly, so the millefeuille should be eaten within a day. Cut the millefeuille with a sharp serrated knife.

White chocolate and raspberry millefeuilles

MILLEFEUILLES AU CHOCOLAT BLANC ET AUX FRAMBOISES

To be enjoyed with a glass of Champagne and Edith Piaf singing 'L'hymne à l'amour' in the background, this is the perfect dessert for a romantic dinner.

Makes 6 / **Preparation time:** 40 + 45 minutes
Resting time in the fridge: 4 hours + 30 minutes
Baking time: 15-20 minutes at 170°C/325°F/Gas Mark 3 / **You will need 2 baking trays**

INGREDIENTS
300g puff pastry
   (see page 12)

*For the white chocolate
   and vanilla mousse*
2 small gelatine leaves
   (3g)
120g white chocolate
200g fresh double cream
1 vanilla pod (opened
   and scraped)
280g fresh double
   cream, softly whipped

For the decoration
icing sugar, to dust
2 large punnets of
   raspberries (125g each)

1. Make the puff pastry following the method on page 12. This step can be done the day before.

2. Make the white chocolate and vanilla mousse (see page 82). This step can also be done the day before.

3. Roll out the puff pastry to a rectangle 2mm thick (30 x 40cm). Rest in the fridge for 30 minutes before baking to prevent it from shrinking.

4. Place the puff pastry between 2 sheets of baking paper, then between 2 baking trays, to stop it from rising excessively. Bake for 12 minutes, then remove the trays from the oven and press down on them using your body weight to flatten it out. Check the colour of the pastry before putting it back in the oven for 6 to 8 minutes to finish baking; it should be evenly golden brown. Cool on a wire rack.

5. With a serrated knife, cut 18 rectangles of approximately 12 x 4cm. I always do one millefeuille at a time (3 rectangles). Divide the pastry into 2 rectangles (15 x 40cm), and then cut 3 strips (15 x 4cm) for the first millefeuille. Place them in front of you lengthways, next to each other, and trim them down to 12cm, cutting both sides of the 3 pieces. Put them aside on top of each other and repeat these steps for the remaining millefeuilles.

6. Fill a piping bag fitted with a medium-size nozzle (square or round) with the white chocolate and vanilla mousse.

7. Assemble a millefeuille with 1 rectangle of puff pastry, a layer of white chocolate mousse, then another rectangle of puff pastry and a layer of raspberries. Dust the final top layer of puff pastry by covering half of it with a sheet of paper placed diagonally and dusting the uncovered pastry with the icing sugar. Remove the sheet of paper carefully to reveal the uncoated pastry and place it on the top of the millefeuille. Decorate with 3 raspberry halves.

Dark chocolate millefeuille

MILLE-FEUILLE TOUT CHOCOLAT

This dessert will please all chocolate lovers – from the pastry to the icing, it's all chocolate.

Serves 10 (1 large millefeuille) / Preparation time: 40 + 35 minutes
Resting time in the fridge: 2½ hours
Baking time: 25-30 minutes at 180°C/350°F/Gas Mark 4 / **You will need 2 baking trays**

INGREDIENTS
For the dough
40g cocoa powder
375g plain flour
75g white bread flour
10g salt
300ml water
1 teaspoon white wine
   vinegar

500g butter

For the millefeuille cream
300g dark chocolate
   (70%), chopped
700ml full fat or
   semi–skimmed milk
5 egg yolks
100g caster sugar
50g plain flour

For the garnish
50g icing sugar
50g cocoa powder

1. Sift the cocoa powder with both of the flours and make the puff pastry following the method on page 12. This step can be done the day before.

2. For the millefeuille cream, put the chopped chocolate in a large bowl. Make the crème pâtissière following the method on page 28. Pass it through a very fine sieve over the chocolate and whisk until melted. Cover with cling film so that it is in contact with the mixture and rest in the fridge for a minimum of 2 hours.

3. Cut the puff pastry into 4 equal parts (only 3 will be used). Roll them out into 4mm-thick rectangles. Remove the excess flour and prick them on both sides with a fork. Rest in the fridge for 30 minutes.

4. Place each sheet of puff pastry between 2 sheets of baking paper, then between 2 trays to stop it from rising excessively. Bake for 20 minutes, then remove the trays from the oven and press on them using your body weight to flatten out the pastry. Turn the trays and put them back in the oven to finish baking for about 5–10 minutes. Cool on a wire rack.

5. One at the time, trim the pastry sheets down with a serrated knife into 3 rectangles (15 x 28cm).

6. Whisk the chocolate millefeuille cream in a large bowl and fill a piping bag fitted with a medium-size nozzle.

7. Assemble the millefeuille: put a first rectangle of puff pastry on a tray, pipe over a layer of cream and cover it up with a second rectangle of pastry. Pipe a second layer of millefeuille cream. To decorate the final layer of puff pastry with icing sugar and cocoa powder, place it on the work surface, put a sheet of paper across diagonally, and sprinkle the uncovered pastry with icing sugar using a sieve. Remove the sheet of paper and slide off the icing sugar. Put it back on the third layer of pastry to cover the icing sugar and sprinkle some cocoa powder on the other side. Slowly remove the paper. Place the pastry carefully on the top of the millefeuille and keep in the fridge.

CHAPTER 5

Choux pastry

LA PÂTE À CHOUX

Chantilly choux

Very easy to make, this is the ideal dessert for a large reception or dinner party. Serve the Chantilly choux with a fresh berry salad or enjoy them on their own with a nice cup of tea.

Makes 20 large choux / **Preparation time:** 20 + 20 minutes
Baking time: 20 minutes at 200°C/400°F/Gas Mark 6 + 15 minutes at 160°C/325°F/Gas Mark 3 to dry out / **You will need a non-stick baking tray**

INGREDIENTS
350g choux pastry
 (^{1}/2 recipe on page 18)
450g Chantilly cream
 (1^1/2 recipe on page 34)
1 beaten egg, to glaze
30g icing sugar

1. Make the choux pastry following the method on page 18, up to step 6.

2. On a non-stick tray, pipe the choux pastry into domes 4cm in diameter, in staggered rows, 6cm apart. Brush them with beaten egg and bake with a small ramekin filled with boiling water (80ml) at the bottom of the oven without opening the oven door (otherwise choux will collapse). Cool on a wire rack.

3. Make the Chantilly cream following the method on page 34, fill a piping bag fitted with a fluted nozzle and keep it in the fridge.

4. Remove the top of the choux with a serrated knife and fill them with the Chantilly cream.

5. Put the lids back on and sprinkle the Chantilly choux with icing sugar using a very fine sieve.

Chocolate éclairs

These éclairs look more complicated to make than they really are. Serve them as a dessert or for afternoon tea. It's a guaranteed success.

Makes 20 large eclairs / **Preparation time:** 20 + 45 minutes / **Resting time in the fridge:** 2 hours
Baking time: 15 minutes at 200°C/400°F/Gas Mark 6 + 20 minutes at 160°C/325°F/Gas Mark 3 to dry out / **You will need a non-stick baking tray**

INGREDIENTS

350g choux pastry
 (¹/₂ recipe on page 18)
1 beaten egg, to glaze

For the chocolate crème pâtissière
150g dark chocolate (55%)
450g crème pâtissière (see page 28)

For the cocoa icing
15g cocoa powder
3 tablespoons water
250g white fondant for millefeuille (or 250g white icing + 30–40ml boiling water)

1. Chop the dark chocolate into small pieces and put it in a large bowl.

2. Make the crème pâtissière following the method on page 28, then pass the hot crème pâtissière thought a sieve over the chopped chocolate and whisk until melted. Cover it with a layer of cling film in direct contact with the cream, and put it in the fridge for a minimum of 2 hours.

3. Make the choux pastry following the method on page 18 up to step 6.

4. On a non-stick baking tray, pipe the choux pastry into 10cm-long batons, in staggered rows 5cm apart. Brush with beaten egg and bake with a ramekin filled with boiling water (80ml) at the bottom of the oven. Do not open the oven during the first 15 minutes of baking otherwise the choux will collapse. Cool on a wire rack.

5. Whisk the chocolate crème pâtissière and fill a piping bag fitted with a medium round nozzle.

6. Turn the éclairs upside down and cut them in half along their sides, keeping one side still attached. Fill them with the chocolate crème pâtissière.

7. For the cocoa icing, mix the cocoa powder with the water to make a paste. Warm up the white fondant (36–37°C) in the microwave, at medium power for 1 minute, and mix it with the cocoa paste. Alternatively, put the white icing in a bowl and warm for 30 seconds in the microwave at medium power (35–40°C). Place it in the bowl of an electric mixer fitted with a paddle, work it with boiling water until the mix softens, then add the cocoa paste. The mix must be runny. Use warm.

8. Glaze the chocolate éclairs with the cocoa icing using a teaspoon on the flat side of the éclairs. Set in the fridge.

Chocolate profiteroles

PROFITEROLES AU CHOCOLAT

I like to vary this recipe by using vanilla whipped cream or mint chocolate-chip ice cream instead of the crème pâtissière. You could also try sprinkling some toasted flaked almonds on top of the chocolate sauce.

Makes 25 / **Preparation time:** 20 + 40 minutes / **Resting time in the fridge:** 2 hours
Baking time: 15 minutes at 200°C/400°F/Gas Mark 6 + 15 minutes at 160°C/325°F/Gas Mark 3 to dry out / **You will need a non-stick baking tray**

INGREDIENTS
450g crème pâtissière
  (page 28)
350g choux pastry
  ($^1/_2$ recipe on page 18)
1 beaten egg, to glaze

For the chocolate ganache
125g dark chocolate
  (64%)
35g butter
60ml full fat or semi-
  skimmed milk
25ml fresh double cream

For the chocolate sauce
150g dark chocolate
200ml full fat or semi-
  skimmed milk

1. Make the crème pâtissière following the method on page 28 and rest in the fridge for 2 hours.

2. Make the choux pastry following the method on page 18 up to step 6.

3. On a non-stick baking tray, pipe the choux pastry into domes 3cm in diameter, in staggered rows 5cm apart to allow them to spread. Brush them with beaten egg and bake with a ramekin filled with boiling water (80ml) at the bottom of the oven. Do not open the oven during the first 15 minutes of baking otherwise the choux will collapse. Cool on a wire rack.

4. Whisk the crème pâtissière and fill a piping bag fitted with a small round nozzle.

5. With the tip of a knife, make a hole at the bottom of each choux and fill with crème pâtissière.

6. To make the ganache, melt the chocolate and butter in the microwave (or in a bain-marie, see page 24), at medium power for 1 minute, then check and stir with a spatula. Repeat this step every 30 seconds until both are melted. Then add the cold milk and cream in 3 or 4 batches. This will make the temperature of the ganache drop. Add an extra 20 seconds in the microwave to warm it up and bring it back to 40°C (it must feel warm but not hot) which is a good temperature to use a ganache. Dip the tops of the profiteroles into the ganache and set in the fridge.

7. For the chocolate sauce, chop the chocolate and put it in a bowl. Bring the milk to the boil, then pour half of it on the top of the chopped chocolate. Stir with a spatula until the chocolate is melted and add the rest of the milk. Serve warm with the profiteroles.

Roc sugar choux

CHOUQUETTES

Light and crispy, they are the children's favourite. If you do get the chance to taste them, I recommend you eat them when they are still warm from the oven, along with a nice cup of coffee.

Makes approximately 60 / **Preparation time:** 25 minutes
Baking time: 14 + 2–4 minutes at 180°C/350°F/Gas Mark 4 / **You will need 2 non-stick baking trays**

INGREDIENTS

For the choux pastry
125ml full fat or semi-
　skimmed milk
125ml water
5g salt
15g caster sugar
110g butter
150g white bread flour
4 medium eggs

For the topping
1 beaten egg, to glaze
50g nibbed sugar

1. Put the milk, water, salt, caster sugar and butter in a saucepan, and follow the method for making choux pastry on page 18, up to step 6.

2. Fill a piping bag fitted with a medium-size nozzle with the choux mixture. On 2 non-stick trays, pipe the pastry into domes 2cm in diameter, in staggered rows, leaving 4cm between them to allow them to spread.

3. Brush them with beaten egg, sprinkle over some nibbed sugar and bake for 14 minutes with a ramekin filled with boiling water at the bottom of the oven, without opening the oven door (otherwise the choux will collapse). Then turn the tray in the oven for another 2–4 minutes. The roc sugar choux must not be too dark. Cool on a wire rack.

Iced coffee cream choux

RELIGIEUSE AU CAFÉ

I'm a coffee girl and I love it when the coffee crème pâtissière is very strong. I find that it balances harmoniously with the sweetness of the coffee icing, and makes these little iced coffee cream choux quite addictive.

Makes 12 / **Preparation time:** 20 + 50 minutes / **Resting time in the fridge:** 2 hours / **Baking time:** 15 minutes at 200°C/400°F/Gas Mark 6 + 15–20 minutes at 160°C/325°F/Gas Mark 3 to dry out / **You will need a non-stick baking tray**

INGREDIENTS
350g choux pastry
  (¹/2 recipe on page 18)
1 beaten egg, to glaze
150g Chantilly cream
  (¹/2 recipe on page 34)

For the coffee crème pâtissière
450g crème pâtissière
  (recipe on page 28)
2–3 teaspoons coffee extract, to taste

For the coffee icing
250g white fondant for millefeuille (or 250g white icing + 30–40ml boiling water)
2 teaspoons coffee extract, to taste

1. Make the crème pâtissière following the method on page 28, and rest in the fridge for 2 hours.

2. Make the choux pastry following the method on page 18, up to step 6.

3. On a non-stick baking tray, pipe the choux pastry in staggered rows into domes 4cm in diameter, 6cm apart for the bases, and 2cm domes, 3cm apart for the tops to allow them to spread. Brush them with beaten egg and bake for 15 minutes at 200°C/400°F/Gas Mark 6 with a ramekin filled with boiling water (80ml) at the bottom of the oven without opening the oven door otherwise the choux will collapse. Transfer the tops to a cooling rack and put the bases back in the oven for 15 minutes at 160°C/325°F/Gas Mark 3. Cool on a wire rack.

4. Whisk the crème pâtissière in a bowl and flavour it with the coffee extract. Fill a piping bag fitted with a small round nozzle.

5. With the tip of a knife, make a hole at the bottom of each choux and fill with the coffee crème pâtissière.

6. For the coffee icing, warm up the white fondant (36–37°C) in the microwave, for 1 minute at medium power. Alternatively, put the white icing in a bowl and warm it (35–40°C) in the microwave at medium power. Put it in the bowl of an electric mixer fitted with a paddle, work the white icing and hot water until the mix softens and becomes runny. Flavour with the coffee extract.

7. Glaze the choux by dipping them into the warm coffee icing. Leave to crystallize at room temperature for 15 minutes. Warm up the coffee icing in the microwave for 30 seconds and build up the choux, using a little bit of icing to stick the bases and tops together. Set in the fridge.

8. Make a Chantilly cream following the method on page 34 and use to decorate the iced coffee cream choux.

How to make a caramel

1. Put the caster sugar in the pan with enough water to make a thick paste. Some white wine vinegar can also be added to the mix to stop the sugar from crystallizing ($^1/_2$ teaspoon).

2. Over a high heat, start cooking without stirring until the sugar syrup starts to colour. A pastry brush dipped in water can be used to clean the edges of the pan and stop the sugar from burning.

3. Finish by cooking over a medium heat until the sugar reaches 155–160°C for a clear caramel.

4. Alternatively, heat to 170–180°C for a darker caramel.

✓ CHEF'S ADVICE

Making caramel involves very high temperatures. Do not touch or taste the caramel while it's still hot. Caramel will continue to cook if it stays in the pan: 20g of butter or 3 tablespoons of water can be added to slow it down. Be careful when adding cold water or butter as the temperature difference could cause the caramel to spit. A clear caramel must be used straight away; it will cool and set rather quickly.

French wedding cake

This is our celebration cake; we eat it in France at weddings, but also at christenings and first communion. These special cakes are made of caramelized choux filled with vanilla crème pâtissière, and decorated with sugared almonds. Some also have a nougatine base and they come in all kinds of shapes.

Preparation time: 20 minutes + 1 hour / **Resting time in the fridge:** 2 hours / **Baking time:** 15 minutes at 200°C/400°F/Gas Mark 6 + 15 minutes at 160°C/325°F/Gas Mark 3 to dry out
You will need 2 non-stick baking trays and a 20cm bowl

INGREDIENTS
1.8kg crème pâtissière (4 x recipe on page 28)
700g choux pastry (see on page 18)
100g sugared almonds

For the caramel
500g caster sugar
150ml water

1. Make the crème pâtissière and rest in the fridge for a minimum of 2 hours.

2. Make the choux pastry following the method on page 18 up to step 6. On 2 non-stick baking trays, pipe it into domes 3cm in diameter, in staggered rows, keeping 4cm between them to allow them to spread. Bake them following the method on page 18. The crème pâtissière and the choux can be made the day before. The choux must then be flashed in the oven for 2 minutes at 180°C/350°F/Gas Mark 4 before use.

3. In a large bowl, whisk the crème pâtissière and fill a piping bag fitted with a small round nozzle. The piping bag will be easier to handle if it's only half filled with cream.

4. With the knife tip, make a hole at the bottom of each choux and fill with crème pâtissière.

5. Oil the outside of a 20cm bowl and turn it upside down on a work surface covered with baking paper. This will act as a guide when building the first layer of choux.

6. Make a clear caramel following the method on page 126. The caramel will need to be warmed up one or twice during the process.

7. Build the first layer of choux. The bottom of the choux must be in contact with the bowl. With one hand, hold the first choux against the bowl and dip the side of a second choux into the caramel with the other hand. Stick them to each other on one side. Dip the side of a third choux into the caramel and stick it to the second one on its other side. Repeat this step with as many choux as you need to complete the first layer.

8. Remove the bowl and finish off the croquembouche by making some smaller layers of caramelized choux, placed on top of each other, following the steps below.

9. Build the second layer of choux. Dip the side of the first choux into the caramel and stick it slightly on the inside of the bottom layer, between 2 choux. The caramel will set almost instantly. Dip half of the side of the second choux and stick it to the bottom layer and the first choux from the second layer. Repeat this step with as many choux as needed to complete the second layer.

10. Repeat step 9 until the croquembouche is complete.

11. Decorate with sugared almonds dipped in the caramel.

✓ CHEF'S ADVICE
The croquembouche will not keep for more than half a day in the fridge. After this time, the caramel will start to melt and weaken the structure, and the choux will become soggy.

Saint-Honoré choux cake

SAINT-HONORÉ

This cake is named after a famous street in Paris: le Faubourg Saint-Honoré. A Chiboust cream is the traditional filling for the cake but a Chantilly cream can be used instead.

Serves 10 / **Preparation time:** 2–3 hours / **Resting time in the fridge:** 2½ + 2 hours
Baking time: 15 minutes at 200°C/400°F/Gas Mark 6 + 20 minutes at 160°C/325°F/Gas Mark 3 to dry out / **You will need 2 non-stick baking trays**

INGREDIENTS
For the pastries
250g puff pastry
  (see page 12)
(Or 250g sweet
  shortcrust pastry,
  page 6)
350g choux pastry
1 beaten egg, to glaze

For the choux filling
450g crème pâtissière
  (see page 28)

For the caramel
  (see page 126)
75ml water
250g caster sugar

For the French meringue
  (see page 36)
3 egg whites (120g)
50g caster sugar

For the Chiboust cream
6 small gelatine leaves
  (9g)
450g hot crème
  pâtissière (see page
  26)
150g French meringue
  (see page 36)

1. Make the puff pastry (see page 12) or sweet shortcrust pastry (see page 6), and the crème pâtissière (see page 28) for the choux filling and place them in the fridge. These steps can be done the day before.

2. Make the choux pastry and fill a piping bag fitted with a medium-size nozzle.

3. Roll out the pastry base in a 20cm circle, 3mm thick, and place it on a baking tray. Prick it with a fork. Pipe a ring of choux pastry all the way around the pastry base, 0.5cm from the side.

4. On a non-stick baking tray, pipe 25 small choux (2cm), in staggered rows, leaving enough space between them to spread. Brush with beaten egg.

5. Bake the Saint-Honoré base and the individual choux together with a ramekin filled with boiling water at the bottom of the oven. Remove the choux 10 minutes before the pastry base and cool on a wire rack.

6. In a large bowl, whisk the crème pâtissière and fill a piping bag fitted with a small round nozzle. With a knife tip, make a hole at the bottom of each choux and fill with crème pâtissière.

7. Make a clear caramel. Dip the tops of 8 choux into the caramel and set them upside down on a tray lined with baking paper. Dip the tops of 8 more choux in the caramel and then in the nibbed sugar and set on the baking paper. Dip the bottom of each choux in caramel and

place them on the cake, alternating the caramelized choux and nibbed sugar-coated choux.

8. To make the crème pâtissière for the Chiboust cream, soak the gelatine leaves in cold water for 10 minutes. Make the crème pâtissière and pass it through a very fine sieve into a large bowl. Whisk in the pressed gelatine leaves. Cover it with cling film in contact with the cream and keep it warm over a bain-marie at 65°C (see page 24).

9. Make a French meringue. Whisk the egg whites using an electric mixer at medium speed. Add the caster sugar at the end to firm the meringue.

10. To make the Chiboust cream, whisk the warm crème pâtissière and combine the French meringue, using a whisk, in 3 or 4 additions. Use while it's still warm.

11. Fill a piping bag fitted with a Saint-Honoré nozzle with the meringue mixture and decorate the cake base. (Or make some quenelles by making oval-shape balls using 2 tablespoons in opposite directions.) Set in the fridge for 2 hours.

✓ CHEF'S ADVICE
The French meringue is made from raw egg whites, which give the Saint-Honoré its unique taste and texture. Therefore the cake is fragile; it should be kept in the fridge and eaten within a day.

Praline choux cake

The circular shape of the Paris-Brest represents the wheels of a bike. This cake is named after the famous French bike race.

Serves 10 / **Preparation time:** 20 + 35 minutes / **Resting time in the fridge:** 1 hour
Baking time: 20 minutes at 200°C/400°F/Gas Mark 6 + 20 minutes at 160°C/325°F/Gas Mark 3 to dry out / **You will need a non-stick baking tray**

INGREDIENTS
40g diced almonds
350g choux pastry
  (¹/₂ recipe on page 18)
1 beaten egg, to glaze
20g icing sugar

For the Paris-Brest cream
375g crème pâtissière
  (see page 28)
140g soft butter
90g praline paste (ready-
  made or see recipe
  page 194)

1. Put the diced almonds in a baking tray and toast them in the oven for 10 minutes at 150°C/300°F/Gas Mark 2. Stir them after 5 minutes.

2. Make the choux pastry following the method on page 18 up to step 6, and fill a piping bag fitted with a medium-size nozzle. On a non-stick baking tray, place a 16cm bowl turned upside down (or something similar). Pipe 2 rings of choux pastry next to each other all the way round the bowl, without touching it. Remove the bowl and add a final ring of choux pastry on the top of the other two rings. Bake with a ramekin filled with boiling water at the bottom of the oven without opening the oven door during cooking or the choux cake will collapse. Cool on a wire rack.

3. Make the crème pâtissière following the method on page 28, and cool in the fridge for 1 hour. It will be used at room temperature to make the Paris-Brest cream.

4. Brush the cold Paris-Brest choux shell with beaten egg and sprinkle over some toasted diced almonds. Flash it in the oven for 2 minutes at 150°C/300°F/Gas Mark 2. Cool on a wire rack.

5. Whisk the crème pâtissière in a large bowl and check its temperature. It should be between 20-25°C. If it's too cold, leave it at room temperature for 30 minutes or put it back in the fridge for 15 extra minutes if it's too warm.

6. Using an electric mixer fitted with a whisk, slowly work the soft butter then add the praline paste. Finally, add the crème pâtissière and gradually turn the speed up to incorporate some air into the cream. Fill a piping bag fitted with a large fluted nozzle.

7. Cut the Paris-Brest choux base in half sideways, fill it with the cream and put its lid back on. Keep in the fridge and take out 30 minutes before serving. Sprinkle with icing sugar.

CHAPTER 6

Rising doughs

LES PÂTES LEVÉES

How to roll up croissants

1. Roll out half of the dough into a long rectangle, 4mm thick and 16cm wide.

2. Remove any excess flour from both sides and, if the dough is sticking to the work surface, sprinkle it with a little flour. Cut the dough into triangles with an 8cm base using a large knife.

3. Lay the triangles with their bases towards you and brush the tops with beaten egg.

4. Roll up each triangle tight from the base to the top and transfer to a tray lined with baking paper. Place the sealed joins underneath the croissants.

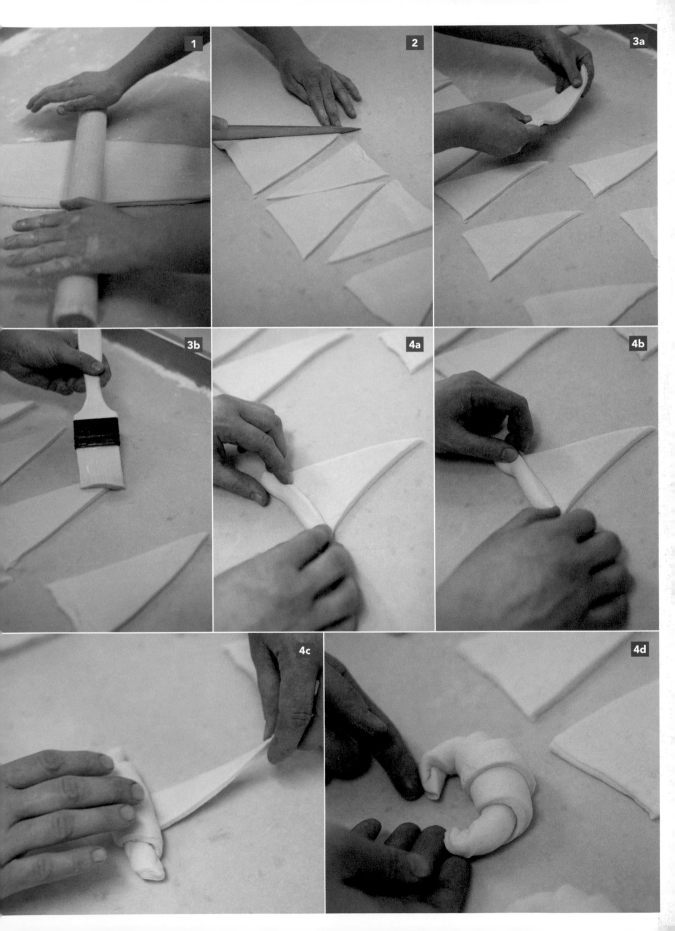

How to roll up almond croissants

1. Roll out half the dough into a long rectangle, 4mm thick and 16cm wide.

2. Remove any excess flour on both sides and if the dough is sticking to the work surface, sprinkle it with little flour. Cut the dough onto triangles with an 8cm base using a large knife (see steps 1 and 2 on page 137).

3. Lay the triangles with their bases towards you and brush the tops with beaten egg. Place batons of marzipan (6 x 0.5cm) at the base of each triangle.

4. Roll up each triangle tight from the base to the top, wrapping up the marzipan in the middle, and transfer them to a tray lined with baking paper. Place the sealed joins underneath the almond croissants.

5. Glaze after baking with white fondant: melt in the microwave for 1 minute at medium power. Or alternatively with white icing: melt in the microwave for 1 minute at medium power and mix with a little hot water. Sprinkle with toasted flaked almonds and set at room temperature.

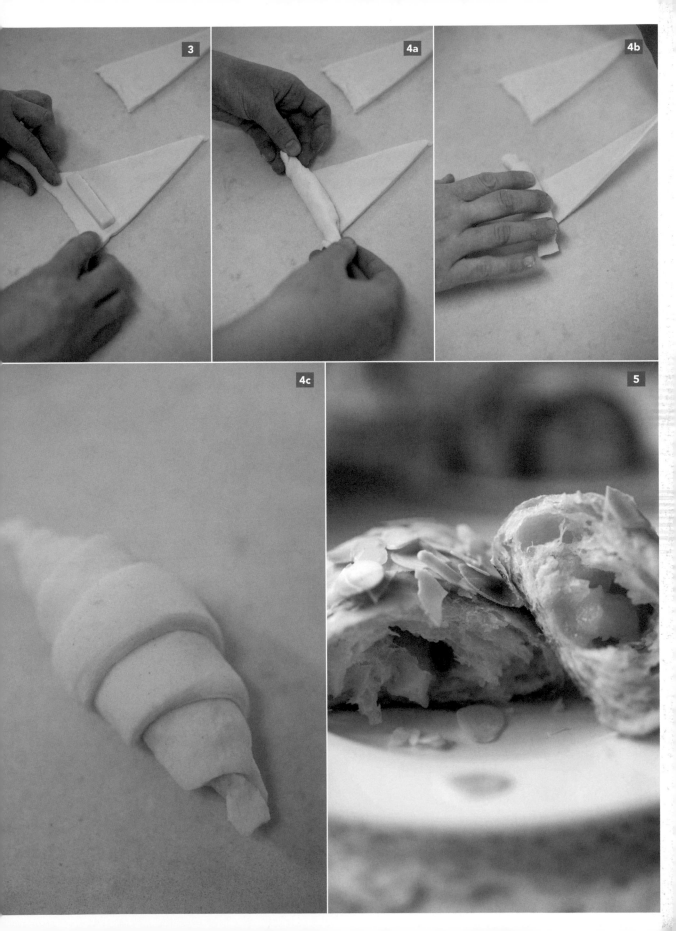

How to roll up pains au chocolat

1. Roll out half the dough into a long rectangle, 4mm thick and 16cm wide.

2. Remove any excess flour on both sides and, if the dough is sticking to the work surface, sprinkle it with a little bit of flour. Place 2 lines of chocolate drops or batons on the top and the bottom of the rectangle, leaving a 1cm gap on each side.

3. Roll up the dough over the chocolate starting from the bottom of the rectangle. And repeat this step with the top of the rectangle.

4. Brush the middle of the dough with beaten egg, and keep rolling up the top and the bottom until it reaches the middle.

5. Turn over the dough and cut into pains au chocolat (roughly every 7cm lengthways) with a large knife. Transfer them to a tray lined with baking paper.

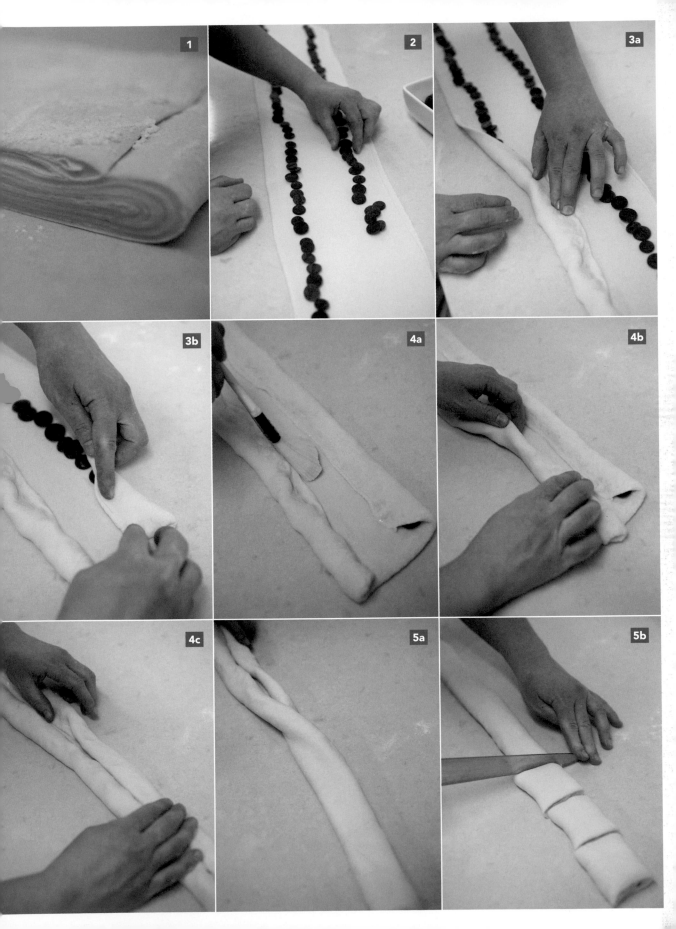

How to roll up pains aux raisins

1. Roll out half of the dough into a square, 4mm thick. Spread over a thin layer of crème pâtissière, leaving a 3cm gap at the top of the dough.

2. Sprinkle the drained macerated raisins over the crème pâtissière.

3. Brush the 3cm gap of dough with beaten egg and roll up the dough starting from the base to the top.

4. Cut the pains aux raisins 2–3cm thick and transfer them on their sides to a tray lined with baking paper.

Croissants, almond croissants, pains au chocolat and pains aux raisins

This recipe will explain to you how to make homemade pastries – and how to organize yourself to have them ready first thing in the morning for breakfast.

Makes approximately 30 / **Preparation time:** 45 + 20 minutes
Proving time for the fresh pastries: 1–1½ hours / **Proving time for the frozen pastries:** overnight
Baking time: 10–12 minutes at 180°C/350°F/Gas Mark 4 / **You will need a non-stick baking tray**

INGREDIENTS

1.1kg croissant dough
(see page 14)
1 beaten egg, to glaze

For the almond croissants
50g marzipan (cut in batons 6 x 0.5cm)
50g toasted flaked almonds (10 minutes at 150°C/300°F/Gas Mark 2)
100g white fondant for millefeuille (or 100g white icing + 15ml boiling water)

For the pains au chocolat
150g dark chocolate drops or batons

For the pains aux raisins
450g crème pâtissière (see page 28)
100g raisins soaked for 1 hour in 50ml dark rum and 50ml boiling water

1. Make the croissant dough following the method on page 14.

2. Sprinkle some flour on the dough and on the work surface. Divide the croissant dough into 2 equal pieces and put 1 in the fridge.

3. Make the croissants following the methods on pages 14 and 136, almond croissants (see page 138), pains aux chocolat (see page 140) and/or pains aux raisins (see page 142).

4. Remove the second piece of dough from the fridge and repeat step 3 to use up all the dough. Freeze the tray of pastries for later use.

5. The evening before, remove as many pastries as you need from the freezer and place them in staggered rows on a non-stick baking tray, 6cm apart, and prove overnight at room temperature (about 20°C). The following morning, brush them with beaten egg and bake for 10–12 minutes at 180°C/350°F/Gas Mark 4. If the pastries have not quite risen enough, start the baking in a cold oven set at 180°C/350°F/Gas Mark 4 and bake for 15–20 minutes.

👍 GOOD TO KNOW

The yeast is fragile and will die if the raw pastries stay in the freezer for too long. I would advise using the frozen pastries within a month.

Parisian brioches

BRIOCHES PARISIENNES

These brioches are only slightly sweet. They are traditionally eaten for breakfast but they could also be served toasted as a starter with foie gras and a nice salade gourmande.

Makes 12 / **Preparation time:** 20 + 20 minutes / **Proving time:** 2–3 hours at room temperature (or overnight in the fridge) + 1–2 hours for the brioches / **Resting time in the fridge:** 1¹/₂ hours (if proved at room temperature) + 15 minutes / **Baking time:** 10–15 minutes at 190°C/375°F/Gas Mark 5 / **You will need 12 x 9cm in diameter brioche moulds**

INGREDIENTS

600g brioche mix
  (see page 20)
1 beaten egg, to glaze

1. Make the brioche dough, prove it for 2–3 hours at room temperature and rest it for 1¹/₂ hours in the fridge. Or prove and rest it overnight in the fridge.

2. Line the brioche moulds with butter and flour. Turn them over and knock them against the work surface to remove the excess flour.

3. Remove the brioche dough from the fridge, turn it over on a lightly floured work surface using a scraper, and press the fermentation gas out using the palms of your hands without working the dough.

4. Cut the dough into 12 individual pieces of 50g. Roll them into balls using the work surface and the palms of your hands. Place them in the fridge for 15 minutes.

5. Stretch out each ball on a work surface using your hand at a 45-degree angle. The smaller side will be used to form the head of the brioche. Then shape the brioche using the side of your hand like a saw, and divide each ball into 2 smaller balls of different sizes connected by a piece of dough in between: the smallest quarter of the dough will be used for the head of the brioche, and the remaining three-quarters will form the body.

6. Put the brioches in their moulds, holding them by their smallest end. Centre the head and push it into the largest part of the brioche using your index fingers.

7. Prove the brioches in a warm place until they double in size (approx 1–2 hours) and brush them with beaten egg.

8. Bake the brioches until golden brown and cool on a wire rack.

5a

5b

6a

6b

Pink praline brioche

BRIOCHE AUX PRALINES ROSES

Pink pralines are caramel-coated almonds. While the brioche is baking, the pink sugar will melt and form a gooey syrup. Don't be afraid to use more than 75g of pink pralines – it's everyone favourite part.

Makes 1 large brioche / **Preparation time:** 20 + 15 minutes / **Proving time:** 2–3 hours at room temperature (or overnight in the fridge) + 1–2 hours for the brioche / **Resting time in the fridge:** 1½ hours (if proved at room temperature) / **Baking time:** 25–30 minutes at 180°C/350°F/Gas Mark 4
You will need a non-stick baking tray

INGREDIENTS
600g brioche mix
  (see page 20)
75g pink pralines
1 beaten egg, to glaze

1. Make the brioche dough, prove it for 4 hours at room temperature and rest it for 1¹/₂ hours in the fridge. Or prove and rest it overnight in the fridge.

2. Crush the pink pralines into small pieces using a large knife and a chopping board, or a food processor.

3. Remove the brioche dough from the fridge, turn it over on a lightly floured work surface using a scraper, and press the fermentation gas out with the palms of your hands without working the dough.

4. Shape it into a rectangle (20 x 30cm) and cut it lengthways into 3 equal parts.

5. With a rolling pin, roll out each piece of brioche in width and sprinkle a line of chopped pink praline across its length, 2cm from the base. Wrap the dough around the pink pralines and finish by rolling it up to form a baguette. Repeat this step with the 2 other parts.

6. Assemble the 3 parts of brioche on a non-stick baking tray. Hide the joins underneath and lay them side by side. Form a plait and put some chopped pralines in the plait's holes.

7. Prove the brioche in a warm place until it doubles in size, then brush it with beaten egg.

8. Bake the brioche until evenly golden brown and cool on a wire rack.

Chocolate Vienna breads

PAINS VIENNOIS AU CHOCOLAT

Delicious served with a hot chocolate for breakfast or as an afternoon snack, the French way is to dip the chocolate Vienna bread in the hot chocolate until it becomes all chocolaty. Children of all ages love them.

Makes 4 x 125g loafs / **Preparation time:** 20 + 15 minutes / **Proving time:** 2–3 hours at room temperature (or overnight in the fridge) + 1–2 hours for the Vienna breads / **Resting time:** 1½ hours in the fridge (if proved at room temperature) / **Baking time:** 12–15 minutes at 180°C350°F/Gas Mark 4 / **You will need a non-stick baking tray**

INGREDIENTS
8g fresh yeast
120ml semi-skimmed or
    full fat milk, at room
    temperature
250g white bread flour
    (T55)
5g salt
25g caster sugar
1 medium egg
30g soft butter, diced

75g dark chocolate
    drops
1 beaten egg, to glaze

1. Make the Vienna bread dough following the brioche method on page 20, incorporating the chocolate drops at the end. Prove it for 2–3 hours at room temperature until the dough doubles in size and rest it for 1½ hours in the fridge, or prove and rest it overnight in the fridge.

2. Remove the dough from the fridge, turn it over on a lightly floured work surface using a scraper, and press the fermentation gas out with the palm of your hands without working the dough.

3. With your hands, shape it into a rectangle(20 x 30cm) and cut it with a knife into 4 equal parts across its width.

4. With a rolling pin, roll out each piece of dough in width. Fold 1cm of the base inside the dough and press gently with your fingertips to seal. Repeat this step with the top end of the dough. Repeat these steps until the bottom part meets the top part. Join them together using your fingertips and roll the dough over using the palms of your hands to form it into a baguette shape. Turn it over onto a non-stick baking tray. Repeat these steps with the 3 other pieces. Place the baguettes, 5cm apart, on the baking tray, hiding the joins underneath.

5. Cut the tops off the baguettes using the tip of a very sharp knife.

6. Prove the chocolate Vienna breads in a warm place until they double in size (1–2 hours) and brush them with beaten egg before baking until brown. Cool on a wire rack.

Kugelhopf

KOUGLOF

This Alsatian brioche is traditionally eaten for family Sunday breakfasts. If you do not own a Kugelhopf mould, you could use a large cake tin or 2 small ones, and sprinkle the flaked almonds at the bottom. This will not affect its amazing taste.

Makes 1 large Kugelhopf / **Preparation time:** 20 minutes / **Resting time in the fridge:** overnight
Proving time: 2–3 hours in a warm place / **Baking time:** 30–40 minutes at 160°C/325°F/Gas Mark 3
You will need a 22 x 11cm silicone mould

INGREDIENTS
20g fresh yeast
210ml full fat or semi-
  skimmed milk, at room
  temperature
500g white bread flour
60g caster sugar
10g salt
2 medium eggs
15ml dark rum
200g soft butter, diced
120g sultanas

For the topping
20g soft butter
10g flaked almonds
20g icing sugar

See the brioche method on page 20

1. Dissolve the fresh yeast in the milk.

2. Put the white bread flour, caster sugar, salt, eggs and dark rum in the mixing bowl. Add the dissolved fresh yeast and work the mix with a dough hook for 10 minutes at slow speed.

3. Add the soft butter and work the dough until it has an even consistency and comes unstuck from the surface of the bowl. Then add the sultanas.

4. With a piece of kitchen paper, spread out a little bit of oil (olive or vegetable) in a large bowl. Place the Kugelhopf dough in its middle and cover the bowl with a wet cloth or cling film. Rest overnight (12 hours) in the fridge.

5. The following day, grease the mould with soft butter and place the flaked almonds at the bottom.

6. Turn over the dough on a floured work surface and remove the fermentation gas using the palm of your hands. Shape it into a circle and make a hole in its middle using 2 fingertips. Fill the mould with the dough and prove in a warm place for about 2 hours until the dough reaches the surface. Bake it until golden brown (on the top and sides) and turn it over onto a wire rack to cool. Sprinkle with icing sugar before serving.

Saint-Tropez tart

TARTE TROPÉZIENNE

Born in Brigitte Bardot's town, the Saint-Tropez tart is now famous everywhere in France.
The Grand Marnier syrup gives it its unique taste – enjoy it with a fresh citrussy drink.

Serves 8 / **Preparation time:** 20 minutes +1¼ hours
Resting time: overnight in the fridge / **Proving time:** 1½–2 hours / **Baking time:** 20–25 minutes at
180°C/350°F/Gas Mark 4 / **You will need a 24cm round cake mould**

INGREDIENTS
300g of brioche dough
   (¹/2 recipe on page 20)
1 beaten egg, to glaze

For the topping (optional)
15g soft butter
20g caster sugar
30g plain flour

For the Saint-Tropez
   cream
200g crème pâtissière
   (see page 28)
200g buttercream
   (see page 32)

For the syrup
1 tablespoon boiling
   water
2 tablespoons caster
   sugar
3 tablespoons Grand
   Marnier

1. The brioche mix and crème pâtissière can be made the day before.
Make the brioche mix following the method on page 20, and store it
in the fridge overnight.

2. Make the crème pâtissière following the method on page 28 and
place in the fridge.

3. On the day, line the mould with butter and flour. Turn it over and
knock it against the work surface to remove any excess flour.

4. Remove the brioche from the fridge, turn it out on a lightly
floured work surface and roll it out to the size of the mould. Remove
the excess flour and place the brioche in the mould. Prove it at room
temperature until it doubles in size and brush it with beaten egg.

5. For the topping (if used), put the soft butter, caster sugar and flour in
a bowl and mix with your fingertips until crumbly. Sprinkle it over the
top of the glazed brioche. Bake it until brown and cool on a wire rack.

6. To make the Saint-Tropez cream, make the buttercream and keep
it at room temperature. In a bowl, work 200g of crème pâtissière with
a whisk and incorporate 200g of the buttercream.

7. For the syrup, mix the boiling water with the caster sugar, then
add the Grand Marnier. Allow 10 minutes for the sugar to dissolve.

8. Cut the brioche in half widthways. Soak the bottom part of the
brioche in syrup using a pastry brush. Spread the Saint-Tropez
cream over the cut side and put the lid back on.

👍 GOOD TO KNOW

Icing sugar can be used instead of the topping (or in addition to
the topping) and sprinkled on the top of the Saint-Tropez tart
just before serving.

Aveyron prune tart

TARTE AUX PRUNEAUX AVEYRONNAISE

This is the traditional dessert from Aveyron, the part of France where I come from. At home, I tend to use an Aubrac tea bag, which is an infusion of local plants, instead of an English breakfast tea bag. It doesn't make a big difference, however, it's just the tradition.

Serves 10 (24cm tart) / **Preparation time:** 20 + 15 minutes / **Proving time:** 2 hours at room temperature + 1 hour in the fridge / **Baking time:** 35–45 minutes at 180°C/350°F/Gas Mark 4
You will need a 24cm tart tin

INGREDIENTS

For the fouace dough
8g fresh yeast
75ml full fat or semi-
   skimmed milk
250g white bread flour
   (T55)
4g salt
85g caster sugar
1 medium egg
1 teaspoon orange-
   flower water
40g soft butter, diced
1 beaten egg, to glaze

For the prune compote
500g stoned dried Agen
   prunes
50g caster sugar
2 pinches of ground
   cinnamon
1 teaspoon vanilla
   extract
1 English breakfast
   teabag
1 tablespoon dark rum

1. Make the fouace dough following the brioche method on page 20. Prove for 2 hours in a warm place, then put in the fridge for 1 hour. Or rest overnight in the fridge.

2. Make the prune compote: put the prunes, caster sugar, ground cinnamon and vanilla extract in a large pan and cover with water. Simmer for 10 minutes, stirring occasionally. Put the tea bag in the pan and infuse for 15 minutes. Drain the prunes and keep the cooking juice to adjust the consistency of the compote. Blitz the prunes with the dark rum in a food processor, gradually adding a little prune cooking juice to lighten the mix. Cool for 1 hour at room temperature.

3. Line the tart tin (see page 42) and cut away the excess pastry with a knife. Spread out the prune compote and make a lattice pattern on top with the leftover dough.

4. Brush the dough with the beaten egg and bake the tart for 25 minutes. Cover it with foil to prevent it from burning and continue to bake for another 10–20 minutes. Cool in the tin.

✓ CHEF'S ADVICE

Serve the Aveyron prune tart with a homemade crème anglaise (see page 26).

Cherry and cinnamon brioche tart

TARTE BRIOCHÉE AUX CERISES

The brioche tart dough is wetter than a brioche dough and a little trickier to roll out, but it works very well with juicy fruits like cherries. When the dough rises in the oven, it will absorb the juice released by the cherries during baking.

Serves 12 (28cm tart) / **Preparation time:** 20 + 20 minutes / **Proving time:** 2–3 hours at room temperature (or overnight in the fridge) / **Resting time:** 1½ hours in the fridge (if proved at room temperature) / **Baking time:** 40–45 minutes at 180°C/350°F/Gas Mark 4
You will need a 28cm tart tin

INGREDIENTS

For the brioche tart dough
10g fresh yeast
45ml milk, at room temperature
220g white bread flour (T55)
4g salt
30g caster sugar
3 small eggs (150g)
80g soft butter, diced

For the garnish
100g demerara sugar
½ teaspoon ground cinnamon
600g stoned black cherries

To serve
Vanilla or cinnamon ice cream

1. Make the brioche tart dough following the method on page 20. Prove for 2-3 hours at room temperature, then put in the fridge for 1½ hours. Or rest overnight in the fridge.

2. Mix the demerara sugar with the ground cinnamon.

3. Turn the dough out on to a floured work surface. The brioche tart is always a little bit sticky. It needs to be rolled out straight from the fridge with more flour than used for a classic pastry. Remove the excess flour with a brush or your fingertips and line the tart tin (see page 42). Cut away the excess dough with a knife.

4. Sprinkle a third of the cinnamon sugar on the pastry base, garnish with the stoned black cherries and sprinkle another third of cinnamon sugar over the fruit.

5. Bake for 25 minutes at 180°C/350°F/Gas Mark 4, then cover the tart with foil and continue to bake for another 20–25 minutes until the pastry base is evenly golden brown. Remove the foil and cool in the mould.

6. Sprinkle with the last third of cinnamon sugar and serve with vanilla or cinnamon ice cream.

Rum baba with vanilla whipped cream

BABA AU RHUM, CRÈME FOUETTÉE À LA VANILLE

My rum baba is a nod to my grandmother. It is in fact a savarin and not a true baba, but that's what she would have called it.

Serves 10 / **Preparation time:** 20 + 15 minutes / **Proving time:** 1–1½ hours in a warm place
Baking time: 25–30 minutes at 180°C/350°F/Gas Mark 4 / **You will need a 20cm savarin mould**

INGREDIENTS
500g savarin dough
(page 22)

For the rum syrup
500ml water
250g caster sugar
1 vanilla pod (opened
and scraped)
50–80ml dark rum, to
taste

For the garnish
100g apricot jam
1 tablespoon water
1 small ripe pineapple

*For the vanilla whipped
cream*
280ml fresh double
cream
20g caster sugar
seeds of 1 vanilla pod

1. Make the baba following the savarin method on page 22.

2. To make the syrup, bring the water, caster sugar and vanilla seeds and pod to the boil. Infuse the vanilla for 20 minutes, pass it through a sieve then add the dark rum, according to your taste.

3. Place the baba on a griddle set over a high-sided large dish. Warm up the syrup (to about 60°C) and pour it over the baba using a ladle. Repeat this step several times until the baba is completely soaked in rum syrup.

4. Warm up the apricot jam with a tablespoon of water and glaze the baba with a pastry brush. Move the baba carefully onto a serving tray.

5. Top and tail the pineapple, and cut off its skin using a large serrated knife. Make a fruit salad with the chopped pineapple and 4 tablespoons of leftover rum syrup and place inside the baba.

6. Before serving, make the vanilla whipped cream following the Chantilly cream method on page 34 and place it on the top of the baba, over the pineapple salad.

Kirsch savarins with cherry compote

SAVARINS AU KIRSCH, COMPOTÉE DE CERISES

Kirsch savarins are less common than the rum ones but they are well worth tasting. Kirsch is a liqueur made from cherries and it works marvellously with cherry compote.

Makes 8 / **Preparation time:** 20 + 15 minutes / **Proving time:** 30 minutes – 1 hour in a warm place
Baking time: 10–12 minutes at 200°C/400°F/Gas Mark 6 / **You will need 8 x 7cm savarin tins**

INGREDIENTS
250g savarin dough
(^{1}/2 recipe on page 22)

For the kirsch syrup
500ml water
250g caster sugar
1 orange zest
1 lemon zest
1 vanilla pod (opened
   and scraped)
40–60ml kirsch, to taste

For the cherry compote
160g caster sugar
15g cornflour
350g cherry purée or
   350ml mixed red berry
   juice or smoothie
350ml red wine
^{1}/2 cinnamon stick
zest and juice of 1 lemon
zest and juice of 1 orange
1 kg of black cherries,
   stoned

For the glaze
100g apricot jam
1 tablespoon water

To serve
300ml crème fraîche or
   vanilla whipped cream

1. Make the individual savarins following the method on page 22.

2. For the cherry compote, mix the cornflour with the caster sugar, then put all the ingredients but the fresh cherries in a pan and bring to the boil. Leave to infuse for 5 minutes off the heat, then pass it through a very fine sieve. Bring the liquid back to the boil with the cherries and cook it gently for 5 minutes. Cool in the pan at room temperature with a piece of greaseproof paper or cling film in contact (to stop the top of the cherries drying out).

3. For the kirsch syrup, bring the water, caster sugar, orange zest, lemon zest and vanilla seeds and pod to the boil. Infuse the zests and vanilla for 20 minutes, pass it through a sieve then add the kirsch, according to your taste.

4. Place the individual savarins upside down in a high-sided dish and pour over the syrup. When they're doubled in size, turn them back up for 15 more minutes. Transfer them to a griddle to remove the excess syrup.

5. Warm up the apricot jam with a tablespoon of water and use to glaze the savarins with a pastry brush.

6. Serve the savarins with the warm cherry compote and a generous tablespoon of crème fraîche or vanilla whipped cream (see page 156).

CHAPTER 7

Flans, creams and egg batters

LES FLANS, CRÈMES ET DESSERTS AUX ŒUFS

Cherry clafoutis

CLAFOUTIS AUX CERISES

This traditional dessert from Limousin (in the centre of France) is really popular in France. It's so simple to make, you don't even have to remove the cherry stones. They actually add some extra flavour to the clafoutis mix. But don't forget to warn your guests about them!

Serves 8 / **Preparation time:** 15 minutes / **Baking time:** 25–35 minutes at 160°C/325°F/Gas Mark 3
You will need a 24cm baking dish

INGREDIENTS
2 medium eggs
4 egg yolks
150g caster sugar
20g plain flour
375ml fresh double
    cream
75ml full fat or semi-
    skimmed milk
1 vanilla pod (opened
    and scraped) or 1
    teaspoon vanilla
    extract

For the garnish
15g butter, for greasing
500g black cherries
20g icing sugar

1. In a large bowl, whisk together the eggs, yolks and caster sugar, then add the plain flour.

2. In a pan, bring the cream, milk and the vanilla seeds and pod to the boil. Pour it slowly on the top of the egg mix, whisking continuously as you do. Pass the clafoutis mixture through a very fine sieve and skim the surface with a ladle.

3. Grease the baking dish with butter and put in the cherries.

4. Pour the clafoutis mix over the cherries and bake it until the mix is set and golden on the top. Cool in the dish at room temperature.

5. Serve slightly warm or at room temperature dusted with icing sugar.

My grandmother's pear clafoutis

CLAFOUTIS AUX POIRES DE MAMIE

This is one of the first family recipes that I learnt. It's very simple and delicious, and can be made with any kind of fruit. When you do it, remember to scrape the inside of the eggshells with your index finger, like my grandmother used to do.

Serves 8 / **Preparation time:** 20 minutes / **Baking time:** 25–35 minutes at 160°C/325°F/Gas Mark 3
You will need a 24cm baking dish

INGREDIENTS
500ml semi-skimmed or
   full fat milk
50g butter
60g plain flour
75g caster sugar
3 medium eggs

For the garnish
15g butter, for greasing
4 ripe Conference pears
20g icing sugar

1. Bring the milk and butter to the boil. Put the flour and caster sugar in a bowl and pour the milk and butter mix slowly over the top, whisking all the time. Add the eggs, then pass it through a very fine sieve and skim it with a ladle.

2. Grease the dish with butter.

3. Peel, cut in half and core the pears. Slice them into 0.5–1cm pieces and place them inside the clafoutis dish.

4. Pour the clafoutis mix over the sliced pears and bake until set and golden brown on top. Cool in the dish at room temperature.

5. Serve slightly warm or at room temperature, dusted with icing sugar.

West Indian flan

After baking, the West Indian flan is divided into 3 layers: the desiccated coconut floats on the top, forming a sponge, a rich and creamy flan lies in the middle and a runny caramel sauce sits at the bottom of the dish.

Serves 8 / **Preparation time:** 20 minutes / **Baking time:** 50 minutes – 1 hour at 140°C/275°F/Gas Mark 1 in a bain-marie (see page 24) / **You will need a 24cm baking dish**

INGREDIENTS
For the caramel
150g caster sugar
50 + 25ml water

For the flan filling
1 small can of
  condensed milk (400g)
380ml semi-skimmed or
  full fat milk
3 medium eggs,
  separated
100g desiccated coconut
2 tablespoons dark rum

1. Make a caramel (170°C) following the method on page 126, then, off the heat and very carefully, add 25ml of water. This will help the caramel to melt during baking. Pour the caramelv evenly over the bottom of the baking dish and leave it to set.

2. In a large bowl, mix the condensed milk with the egg yolks, then add the milk, desiccated coconut and dark rum.

3. In a electric mixer on medium speed, whisk the egg whites to a peak (see page 38). Incorporate a third of the egg whites with the flan filling, followed by the last two-thirds without overworking it, making a circular movement from the bottom upwards with the spatula in one hand, giving a quarter turn to the bowl with the other. Keep doing this until the mix is combined.

4. Pour the flan filling in the dish, over the set caramel. Bake it in a bain-marie (see page 24) by placing the flan dish in the oven inside a larger high-sided tray filled with 3cm of boiling water. Check after 45 minutes by gently shaking the flan dish. The flan is cooked when the coconut sponge on the top of the flan is set. Cool at room temperature.

French toast

Delicious, fast and cheap, this is the perfect comfort food, or serve it as a posh breakfast for all the family. Stale bread is commonly used in France instead of the brioche: there are always some pieces of leftover baguette which need to be used up!

Serves 4 / **Preparation time:** 20 minutes / **Cooking time:** 5 minutes
You will need a medium-size frying pan

INGREDIENTS
6 medium eggs
60g caster sugar
1 vanilla pod (opened and scraped) or 1 teaspoon vanilla extract
150ml semi-skimmed or full fat milk
75g fresh double cream
8 thick slices of brioche, cut into halves
30g butter

For the topping
icing sugar, to dust
strawberry jam and fresh strawberries to serve

1. In a bowl, whisk the eggs with the caster sugar and the vanilla (seeds and pod or extract), then add the milk and cream to make a batter.

2. Place the brioche halves flat in the dish and pour over the batter through a very fine sieve. Soak the brioche for a few minutes until the batter soaks into it, then turn them over.

3. Melt a knob of butter in a frying pan. Remove the brioche carefully from the dish, one at a time, and hold it between your fingers for a few seconds to drain the excess butter. Cook them at a medium heat in batches until they are golden brown. Turn them over to finish off the cooking.

4. Sprinkle the French toast with icing sugar and serve warm with strawberry jam and fresh strawberries.

How to make a pancake mix

1. In a large bowl, put the plain flour, caster sugar and salt.

2. Make a well in its middle and add the eggs.

3. Whisk the eggs in the well and add a small quantity of milk.

4. Start whisking from the middle of the well and gradually incorporate some flour.

5. Keep whisking and incorporate alternately some flour from the side of the well and a little more milk in order to make a thick paste. This method will avoid the formation of lumps.

6. When the flour is completely mixed, add the rest of the milk followed by the fresh double cream.

7. Add the hot melted butter and blitz with a hand blender.

8. Rest in the fridge for 30 minutes before cooking. Whisk for 1 minute before use and check its consistency. Add an extra 30–50ml of milk if the mixture has become thicker.

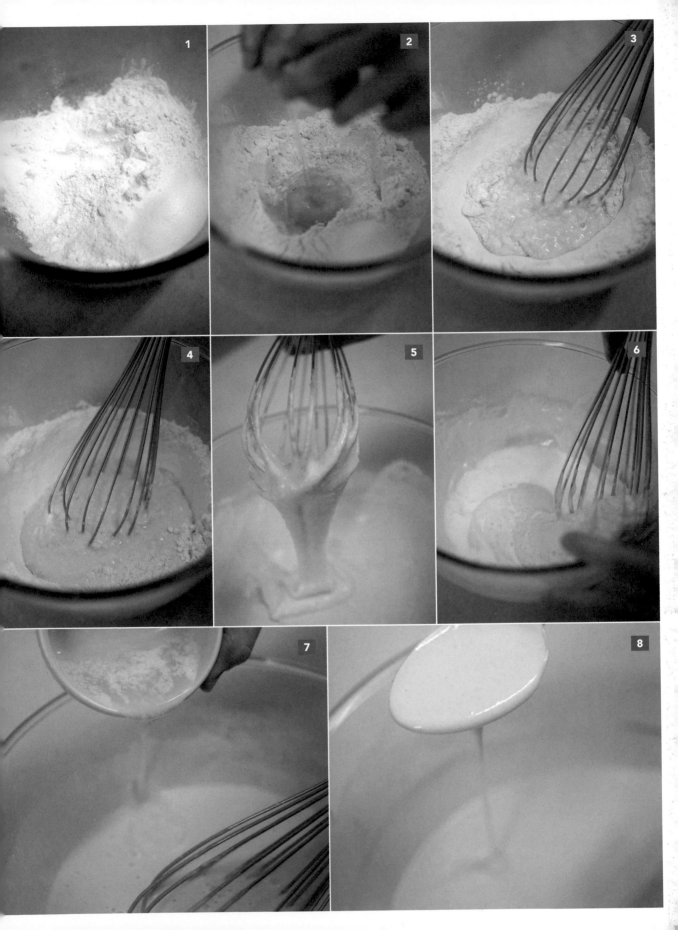

Orange and Grand Marnier pancakes

CRÊPES SUZETTE

Usually, the Grand Marnier is poured over the pancake at the end of the recipe, in a very hot pan, and flambéed right away in front of the guests. But this stage is not necessary if you don't feel confident.

Serves 4 / **Preparation time:** 15 minutes / **Resting time in the fridge:** 30 minutes (or overnight without the caster sugar) / **Cooking time:** 20 minutes (1–2 minutes each pancake) + 5 minutes for the caramel / **You will need a 24cm pancake pan or frying pan**

INGREDIENTS

For the pancake mix
150g plain flour
20g caster sugar
$^1/_2$ teaspoon salt
2 medium eggs
320ml full fat milk
20ml fresh double cream
40g melted butter
30g butter, for greasing

For the orange caramel
60g caster sugar
20g butter
The juice of 2 oranges
40ml Grand Marnier

1. Make the pancake mix following the method on page 174.

2. Grease the pancake pan with a small piece of butter and remove the excess with some kitchen paper. Pour a small ladle of mix into the hot pan and spread it out by tilting the pan. Cook the pancake for 30 seconds to 1 minute until it starts to colour and turn it over using a spatula.

3. Grease the pan using the same kitchen paper and eventually some more butter, and finish off cooking the rest of the pancake mix. Pile them on top of each other to keep them warm. Fold the pancakes into quarters and wipe the pan clean.

4. To make the orange caramel, sprinkle the caster sugar in the pan, put it over a medium heat and make a dry caramel by melting the caster sugar for a few minutes until it becomes brown. Turn down the heat and stir in the butter followed by the orange juice and the Grand Marnier.

5. Put the pancakes back in the pan (4 or 8 at a time, depending on size) and reduce the orange caramel for 1 or 2 minutes before serving. (Alternatively, warm up the pancakes in the microwave and pour over the reduced orange caramel.)

Floating islands

Traditionally, the egg whites are poached in the milk that will be used to make the crème anglaise, or baked in ramekins in a bain-marie (see page 24), but the modern way now is to use the microwave. It's so fast and easy – just brilliant!

Serves 6 / **Preparation time:** 15 + 15 minutes / **Cooking time:** 5 + 15 minutes
Cooling time: 30 minutes for the crème anglaise

INGREDIENTS
400g crème anglaise
  (see page 26)
50g flaked almonds

For the French meringue
2 egg whites (80g)
50g caster sugar

1 tablespoon vegetable
  or olive oil

For the caramel
125g caster sugar
40ml water

1. Make the crème anglaise.

2. Put the flaked almonds on a baking tray and toast them in the oven for 10 minutes at 150°C/300°F/Gas Mark 2. Stir them after 5 minutes.

3. Make a French meringue by whisking the egg whites to a soft peak (see page 38) and gradually incorporate the caster sugar. Carry on whisking until stiff peaks form.

4. Oil 2 plates and shape the French meringue into egg forms using 2 tablespoons. Make 12 portions (6 on each plate). Cook them for 30 seconds in the microwave at maximum power (900W) and cool at room temperature.

5. Fill a large serving bowl or 6 individual dishes with the crème anglaise and place the cooked egg whites on the top.

6. Make a caramel (not too dark) following the method on page 126 and spoon it over the top of the floating islands. Sprinkle with toasted flaked almonds just before serving.

Earl Grey crème brûlée

CRÈME BRÛLÉE AU THÉ EARL GREY

The flavour of the Earl Grey tea is preserved in a cold infusion overnight. This will prevent the crème brûlée from tasting too tannic and allow the black tea and bergamot to express their true flavours.

Serves 8 / **Preparation time:** 20 minutes / **Infusion time in the fridge:** 12 hours (overnight)
Baking time: 50 minutes – 1 hour at 110°C/225°F/Gas Mark ¼ in a bain-marie (see page 24)
Cooling time in the fridge: 4 hours / **You will need 8 x 8cm ramekins and a high-sided baking tray**

INGREDIENTS

300ml semi-skimmed or full fat milk

650ml fresh double cream

35g loose Earl Grey tea leaves

8 egg yolks

110g caster sugar

40g caster sugar to caramelize

1. The night before, put the milk and cream in a bowl and stir in the loose Earl Grey tea leaves. Cover the bowl with cling film and place it in the fridge for 12 hours to make a cold infusion.

2. The following morning, pass the Earl Grey infusion though a double muslin or a fine cloth.

3. In a large bowl, whisk the egg yolks with the caster sugar for 1 minute. Bring the sieved milk, cream and tea infusion to the boil and poor it slowly on the top of the yolks and caster sugar, stirring continuously.

4. Pass the crème brûlée mix through a very fine sieve and skim the surface using a ladle or a tablespoon.

5. Place 8 ramekins in a high-sided baking tray and fill them with the mix. Pour 3cm of boiling water into the bottom of the tray and bake the crèmes brûlées in a static (fan turned off) oven. Alternatively, cling film the baking tray with a heat-resistant cling film all the way around to make it airtight and bake them in a fan oven.

6. After 45 minutes, shake the tray gently, and keep checking every 5 minutes until the cream is set like a jelly, gently moving in the middle. (Remove the cling film). Cool in the tray for 15 minutes at room temperature then put the crèmes brûlées in the fridge for 4 hours.

7. Dry the top of the crèmes brûlées with kitchen paper if needed, cover them with a thin layer of caster sugar and caramelize them using a blowtorch.

✓ CHEF'S TOP TIP

Serve with Bretons biscuits (page 238), flaked almond tuiles (page 234) or finger biscuits (page 242).

My mother's crème caramel

CRÈME CARAMEL DE MA MAMAN

Crème caramels are very easy to make. My mother makes them at least once a month and likes to use fresh farm milk. They can be eaten straight from the ramekin or turned upside down on a plate.

Serves 8 / **Preparation time:** 20 minutes / **Cooking time:** 5 minutes / **Baking time:** 20–30 minutes at 140°C/275°F/Gas Mark 1 in a bain-marie (see page 24) / **Cooling time at room temperature:** 3 hours / **You will need 8 x 8cm ramekins and a high sided-baking tray**

INGREDIENTS
For the caramel
150g caster sugar
50 + 25ml water

For the crème caramel filling
500ml full fat milk
1 tablespoon vanilla extract
2 medium eggs
65g caster sugar

1. Place the 8 ramekins in a high-sided baking tray.

2. For the caramel, make a slightly dark caramel (170-175°C) following the method on page 126, then add 25ml of water off the heat to slow down the cooking. This will help the caramel to melt during baking. Be careful when adding the water as the caramel will spit.

3. Pour the caramel into the ramekins straight away as it will continue to cook if left in the pan.

4. To make the crème caramel filling, in a large bowl, whisk the eggs with the caster sugar. In a pan, bring the milk and vanilla extract to the boil and pour it over the eggs and caster sugar while whisking. Pass it though a very fine sieve and fill the ramekins.

5. Pour 3cm of boiling water into the bottom of the baking tray and cook the crème caramels in a bain-marie (see page 24) for 20–30 minutes at 140°C/275°F/Gas Mark 1 until it is set like a jelly. Cool at room temperature.

✓ CHEF'S TOP TIP
Serve the crème caramel with crisp cinnamon biscuits (page 252) or Nini's sablés (page 240).

Dark chocolate and orange mousse

MOUSSE AU CHOCOLAT NOIR À L'ORANGE

Using 55% dark chocolate will stop the mousse from setting hard in the fridge. If you want to use a darker chocolate, I would recommend you add an extra egg and 30ml of fresh double cream to the original recipe. You can also change its flavour by adding a few drops of mint or coffee extract instead of the orange peel. Or just enjoy it plain.

Serves 6 / **Preparation time:** 15 minutes / **Setting time in the fridge:** 2 hours
You will need 6 medium-size glasses or cups as serving dish

INGREDIENTS
180g 55% dark
  chocolate
120ml fresh double
  cream
30ml semi-skimmed or
  full fat milk
zest of 1 orange (peeled)
20g soft butter
3 medium eggs
20g caster sugar

1. Chop the dark chocolate and put it in a large bowl.

2. In a pan, bring the cream, milk and orange zest to the boil, and pour it over the chocolate through a sieve. Stir with a spatula until the chocolate is completely melted.

3. Dice the soft butter and stir it into the mix.

4. Whisk the 3 egg whites and caster sugar to firm peaks (see page 38) and add the 3 egg yolks at the end.

5. Incorporate one-third of the egg mix to the chocolate, making a circular movement from the bottom upwards with the spatula in one hand, and giving a quarter turn to the bowl with the other. Then fold in the remaining two-thirds of the egg mix.

6. Fill the 6 individual dishes and set them in the fridge for a minimum of 2 hours. Take them out of the fridge 15 minutes before serving.

✓ CHEF'S TOP TIP

Serve the dark chocolate and orange mousse with plain crunchy biscuits such as rolled (page 244), Bretons (page 238) or heart-shaped biscuits (page 250).

Coffee, vanilla and chocolate bavarois

BAVAROIS CAFÉ, VANILLE ET CHOCOLAT

This is a very old-fashioned dessert. The combination of coffee, vanilla and chocolate is always a winner. Classics are timeless, but I did use less gelatine leaves than is traditionally used in this kind of dessert.

Serves 8 / **Preparation time:** 45 minutes / **Resting time at room temperature:** 30 minutes
Resting time in the fridge: 15 x 2 minutes (between layers) / **Cooking time:** 5 minutes
You will need 8 serving glasses + 8 mugs or glasses

INGREDIENTS
8 small gelatine leaves
  (12g)

For the crème anglaise
4 egg yolks
120g caster sugar
125ml semi–skimmed or
  full fat milk
175ml fresh double
  cream
2 vanilla pods (opened
  and scraped)

For the 3-flavour bavarois
  cream
500ml fresh double
  cream
50g dark chocolate
  (64%), chopped
50ml fresh double cream
1 or 2 teaspoons coffee
  extract

1. Soak the gelatine leaves in cold water for 10 minutes.

2. Make the crème anglaise following the method on page 26. Press the gelatine leaves between your hands to remove the excess water and add them to the crème anglaise. Stir with a whisk and cool at room temperature for 30 minutes.

3. Make the bavarois cream: whisk 500ml of cream into a soft and runny whipped cream. Pour it over the crème anglaise and mix with a spatula.

4. Chop the chocolate and put it in a large bowl. Bring the 50ml of cream to the boil and pour it over the chocolate. Stir with a spatula until it is melted. Weigh out 300g of the bavarois cream and incorporate it into the chocolate mix, starting with a small quantity. Pour the chocolate bavarois cream into a jug or a piping bag.

5. Place the 8 serving glasses over 8 other glasses or mugs, at a 45-degree angle, and pour in the chocolate bavarois cream. Set in the fridge for 15 minutes.

6. Stir the remaining bavarois cream and weigh out 350g in a jug or piping bag, to use it as it is for the vanilla layer.

7. Remove the glasses from the fridge, rotate them one-third to the right and pour in the vanilla bavarois. Set in the fridge for 15 minutes.

8. Flavour the remaining 350g bavarois cream with 1 or 2 teaspoons of coffee extract, to taste. Remove the glasses from the fridge, put them flat on the work surface and top with the coffee bavarois. Put in the fridge and remove 15 minutes before serving.

Lemon soufflé

SOUFFLÉ AU CITRON

I'm a little bit fussy when it comes to soufflés; I find that they sometimes taste too eggy, which is why I love this recipe – the lemon crème pâtissière gives the soufflés their incredibly rich taste and very light texture. Just amazing!

Serves 6 / **Preparation time:** 30 minutes / **Cooking time:** 5 minutes / **Resting time in the fridge:** 1 hour / **Baking time:** 8–10 minutes at 180°C/350°F/Gas Mark 4 / **You will need 6 ramekins**

INGREDIENTS

For the lemon crème pâtissière
350ml full fat or semi-skimmed milk
zest of 1 lemon
4 egg yolks
50g caster sugar
25g plain flour
150ml sieved lemon juice (2–3 lemons)

For the mould
30g soft butter
30g caster sugar

For the soufflé mix
260g lemon crème pâtissière
2 egg yolks
4 egg whites
60g caster sugar

1. Bring the milk with the lemon zest to the boil and make the crème pâtissière following the method on page 28. Stir in the lemon juice, cover with cling film in contact with the surface of the cream and place in the fridge for a minimum of 1 hour.

2. Brush the ramekins with soft butter and put them in the fridge for 15 minutes. Brush with butter a second time and coat with caster sugar.

3. For the soufflé mix, in a large bowl, put 260g of lemon crème pâtissière and whisk in the egg yolks. Using an electric mixer at medium speed, whisk the egg whites to a soft peak (see page 38) and gradually add the caster sugar. Whisk the meringue to peak (see page 38). Fold a third of the whipped egg whites into the lemon mix, then the remaining two-thirds, making a circular movement from the bottom upwards with the spatula in one hand, and giving a quarter turn to the bowl with the other.

4. Fill the ramekins using a tablespoon or a piping bag fitted with a large nozzle. Flatten them out with a pallet knife and wipe clean the top of each ramekin using your index finger. Bake and serve straight away.

✓ CHEF'S TOP TIP

The soufflé mix, raw and baked, is quite fragile and will collapse rather quickly. They must be made, baked and served straight away. It is delicious on its own or served with fresh raspberries, a strawberry salad or a cherry sorbet.

CHAPTER 8

Sponge cakes

LES PÂTES À BISCUIT

Apricot jam roulade cake

BISCUIT ROULÉ À LA CONFITURE D'ABRICOT

This very light, butter-free cake is really easy and fast to make; it will save you from any last-minute birthday cake emergencies and both children and parents love it. You can vary the flavour of the jam or use a chocolate and hazelnut spread instead.

Serves 8 / **Cooking time:** 5 minutes (for jam) / **Preparation time:** 30 minutes
Baking time: 10–12 minutes at 180°C/350°F/Gas Mark 4 **You will need a 30 x 40cm baking tray**

INGREDIENTS
450g génoise mix
(see page 24)

For the homemade apricot jam
300g ripe apricots, stoned and diced
180g granulated sugar
(Or 1 small jar of apricot jam)

1. To make the apricot jam, place the diced apricots and granulated sugar in a pan. Bring it to the boil over a medium heat, and cook it for 5 minutes, stirring continuously. Cool at room temperature.

2. Make the génoise sponge mixture following the method on page 24.

3. Spread it out evenly to 8mm–1cm thick on a tray lined with a silicone mat or baking paper. If the sponge is too thick it might tear when you make the roulade. Bake it straight away, turning the tray in the oven after 7–8 minutes to finish baking until golden brown.

4. While the sponge is still hot, use the tip of a knife to separate it from the tray and turn it upside down onto a clean kitchen cloth. Remove the tray and carefully peel away the silicone mat or the baking paper. Place the rectangle sponge with the wider edge facing you and trim each side with a knife to remove the dry parts.

5. Spread over a generous layer of apricot jam, leaving 3cm jam-free at the top edge.

6. Make the roulade by starting to roll from the bottom of the rectangle to the top. Use the cloth to lift up and hold the sponge while rolling. The beginning of the roll must be tight in order to get a perfectly round roulade cake. Finish with the join underneath.

👍 GOOD TO KNOW

The apricot jam can be stored in jars and kept up to a year in a cellar or a cool, dark place. The jars must be filled to the top straight after cooking, while the jam is still boiling hot. Place the lids on and turn the jars upside down in order to sterilize the air inside them. The following day, turn them the right way up and store them.

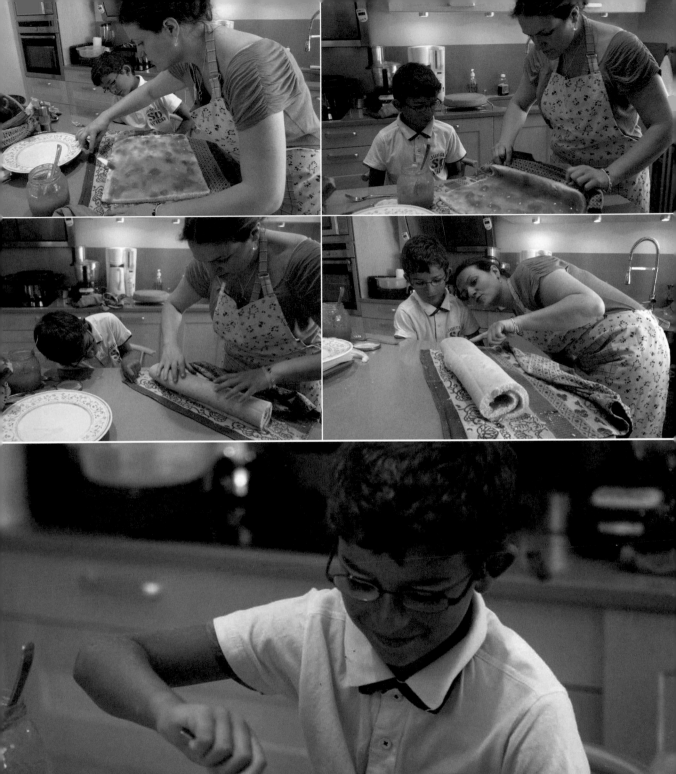

How to make a homemade praline paste

1. Put the blanched almonds and the blanched hazelnuts in a baking tray, and toast them in the oven for 10 minutes at 150°C/300°F/Gas Mark 2. Shake the tray in the oven after 5 minutes to even up the baking.

2. Put the caster sugar and water in a large pan and bring them to the boil at a high heat. Cook the syrup to 115°C using a probe or a sugar thermometer.

3. Add the toasted nuts and turn the heat down.

4. Stir with a spatula; the sugar will crystallize and coat the nuts.

5. Keep stirring at a low heat until the sugar caramelizes evenly without burning. Cool on baking paper.

6. Blitz the caramelized nuts in a food processor for 10–15 minutes.

7. The praline paste must be runny, almost liquid, warm but not hot. Keep it in the fridge. As the natural fat content of the nuts tends to separate and rise to the top, stir the paste before use.

Praline Christmas log

BÛCHE DE NOËL AU PRALINÉ

This pâtisserie is eaten in France on Christmas day. The classic Christmas logs are made with a sponge biscuit and a flavoured buttercream. But all sorts of sweet variations can now be found: trio of ice creams and sorbets, or fruits and mousse Christmas logs.

Serves 10 / **Preparation time:** 1½ hours / **Cooking time:** 5 + 10 minutes
Baking time: 10–12 minutes at 180°C/350°F/Gas Mark 4 / **You will need a 30 x 40cm baking tray**

INGREDIENTS

For the homemade praline paste
150g blanched almonds
150g blanched hazelnuts
85g caster sugar
50ml water

For the syrup
60g caster sugar
40ml water

For the sponge
450g génoise mix (see page 24)

For the praline buttercream
550g buttercream (see page 32)
80g praline paste (homemade or readymade)

For the decoration
150g diced hazelnuts
42g caster sugar
24ml water
10g grated white chocolate

1. Make the homemade praline paste, if using, following the method on page 194.

2. For the syrup, in a pan, bring the caster sugar and the water to the boil. Cool at room temperature.

3. Make the génoise sponge mix. Spread it out evenly to 8mm–1cm thick on a tray lined with a silicone mat or baking paper. If the sponge is too thick it might tear when you roll up the Christmas log. Bake it for 7 minutes, turn the tray in the oven and bake for another 3–5 minutes until golden brown.

4. With a knife tip, separate the sponge from the baking tray. Turn the warm génoise over onto a clean kitchen cloth and peel off the baking paper or the silicone mat. Brush with the syrup while it's warm and trim each side of the sponge with a knife to remove the dry parts.

5. Make the buttercream following the recipe on page 32, but without the vanilla pods. Set aside 2 tablespoons of plain buttercream to garnish the inside of the branch, and incorporate the remainder with the praline paste.

6. Put the diced hazelnuts on a baking tray and toast them for 15 minutes at 150°C/300°F/Gas Mark 2, shaking the tray every 5 minutes. Caramelize the hazelnuts following steps 2–5 of the praline paste method on page 194. Cool on baking paper and break them down by hand.

7. Place the sponge with one of the widest edges facing you and spread over a thin layer of praline buttercream, leaving the top edge 3cm free of cream.

8. Roll the Christmas log starting from the bottom of the rectangle.

The beginning of the roll must be tight in order to get a perfectly round Christmas log. Finish with the join underneath the cake.

9. Slice off a small piece of the Christmas log on the diagonal, place it on the top to make a branch and cover its middle with the plain buttercream. Cover the rest of cake with hazelnut buttercream and use a fork to decorate it. Coat the sides with caramelized hazelnuts and grate some white chocolate over the top for the snow. Keep in the fridge and leave for 15 minutes at room temperature before serving.

Coffee moka

This is definitely one of my favourite cakes. I just love the contrast between the light génoise sponge and the rich coffee buttercream. I recommend keeping the leftover diced almonds and sprinkling them on each slice of cake. It's super delicious this way.

Serves 8 / **Preparation time:** 20 + 35 minutes / **Cooking time:** 5 minutes
Baking time: 25–30 minutes at 160°C/325°F/Gas Mark 3
You will need a 20cm square or round cake tin

INGREDIENTS
450g génoise mix
 (see page 24)

For the coffee buttercream
275g plain buttercream
 ($^1/_2$ recipe see page 32)
1–2 tablespoons coffee
 extract
(or 1 teaspoon instant
 coffee + 1 teaspoon
 boiling water)

For the garnish
150g diced almonds

For the coffee syrup
5 teaspoons caster sugar
1 short espresso or
 strong, short instant
 coffee

1. Make the génoise sponge mix following the method on page 24, bake it and leave it to cool down.

2. Make the buttercream following the method on page 32, and flavour it with the coffee extract to taste. Keep it at room temperature.

3. Put the diced almonds on a baking tray and toast them in the oven for 10 minutes at 150°C/300°F/Gas Mark 2. Stir them after 5 minutes and carry on baking.

4. Make the coffee syrup by adding the caster sugar to the hot coffee.

5. Turn the génoise upside down and split it sideways in 2 equal layers. Soak the inside of the bottom part with the coffee syrup using a pastry brush, then spread over a layer of coffee buttercream (7mm–1cm thick). Soak the inside of the top part of the génoise with the coffee syrup and place it on the top of the buttercream.

6. Spread some coffee buttercream all over the moka, smoothing it on top with a long spatula or knife. Coat its sides with the toasted diced almonds.

7. Fill a piping bag fitted with a small fluted nozzle with the rest of the coffee buttercream and decorate the top of the moka.

✓ CHEF'S ADVICE
The moka must be kept in a cool place or in the fridge, and taken out 30 minutes before serving. The buttercream tastes better served cool but not cold.

Baked Alaska

OMELETTE NORVÉGIENNE

It's the contrast between the cold ice cream and the hot meringue that makes this dessert special. The whipped egg whites do not conduct heat well, which allows the Alaska to be baked for a few minutes without melting the ice cream. It's a scientific 'magic trick'!

Serves 8 / **Preparation time:** 20 + 40 minutes / **Resting time in the fridge:** overnight / **Baking time:** 15–20 minutes at 180°C/350°F/Gas Mark 4 for the sponge, 2 minutes at 250°C/480°F/Gas Mark 9 for the meringue (optional) / **You will need a 20cm oval cake tin and a 20cm oval bowl or a 24cm rectangle cake tin**

INGREDIENTS
225g génoise
  (¹/₂ recipe on page 24)

For the vanilla ice cream
  (you can also use
  ready-made ice cream)
8 egg yolks
80g caster sugar
250ml semi-skimmed or
  full fat milk
350ml fresh double
  cream
1 tablespoon glucose
  syrup

For the syrup
1 tablespoon boiling
  water
2 tablespoons caster
  sugar
3 tablespoons Grand
  Marnier

For the French meringue
  (see page 36)
3 egg whites (120g)
200g caster sugar

1. The day before, make the vanilla ice cream following the crème anglaise recipe on page 26. Add the glucose syrup at the end, off the heat. Rest overnight in the fridge and churn it in an ice-cream maker the next morning. Alternatively you can of course use ready-made ice cream.

2. On the day, make a génoise sponge following the method on page 24, and leave it to cool down.

3. For the syrup, bring the water and caster sugar to the boil, cool for 15 minutes and add the Grand Marnier.

4. Brush the génoise with Grand Marnier syrup. Fill the bowl or tin with vanilla ice cream, place the génoise on top and set it in the freezer for a minimum of 12 hours.

5. Before serving make the French meringue by whisking the egg whites with the caster sugar to peak.

6. Place the ice-cream cake bowl/tin in a larger bowl filled with hot water for a few seconds and turn it out.

7. Spread over the meringue with a spatula and place the cake in a very hot oven (250°C/480°F/Gas Mark 9) for 2 minutes. Or burn the meringue with a blowtorch. Serve straight away.

How to flambé a Baked Alaska
Baked Alaska can be flambéed with Grand Marnier in front of your guests. Warm up 50ml of Grand Marnier in a pan, light it carefully and pour it over the Baked Alaska. It looks quite spectacular and tastes really good, but on the downside it tends to burn the meringue and make it a bit soggy.

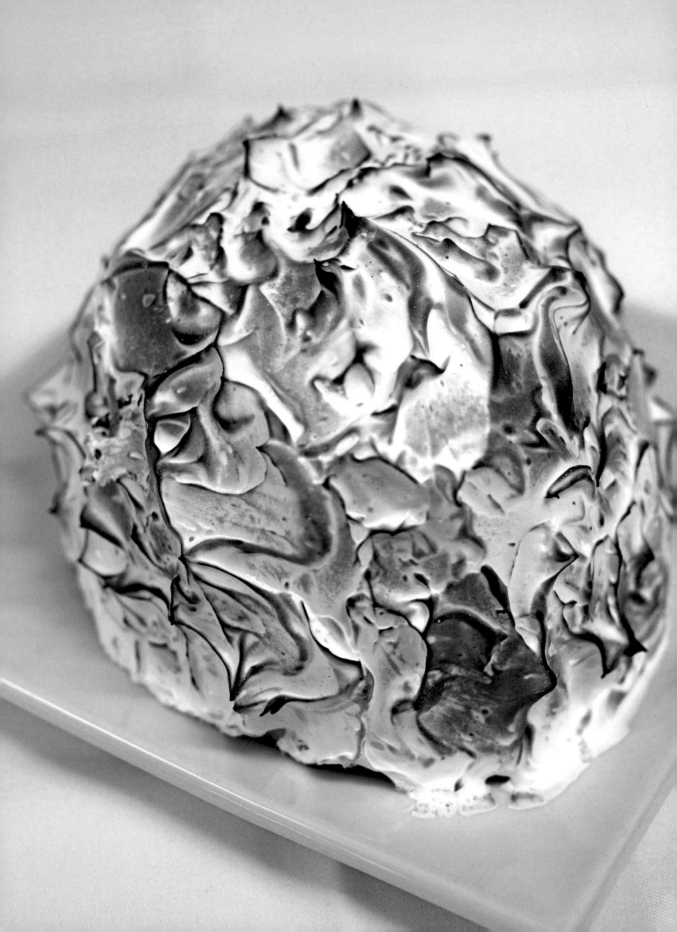

Strawberry and pistachio cream sponge

FRAISIER À LA PISTACHE

This cake is usually made with a vanilla cream prepared with half buttercream and half crème pâtissière. My pistachio Fraisier is a delicious modern take on a classic French cake.

Serves 12 / **Preparation time:** 20 + 40 minutes / **Baking time:** 10–12 minutes at 180°C/350°F/Gas Mark 4 / **Setting time in the fridge:** 8 hours / **You will need a 20 x 6cm ring, a baking tray and a blowtorch**

INGREDIENTS
450g of génoise mix
  (see page 24)

For the kirsch syrup
25g caster sugar
50ml water
2 tablespoons kirsch or
  strawberry liqueur

For the garnish
250g marzipan
30g icing sugar, to dust
2 punnets of large
  strawberries (500g
  each)
25g white chocolate,
  melted

For the pistachio cream
4 small gelatine leaves
  (6g)
30g caster sugar
15ml water
500ml fresh double
  cream
80–100g pistachio paste,
  to taste (readymade or
  homemade, follow
  method for praline
  paste page 194,
  without doing step 1)

1. Make the génoise mix folowing the method on page 24, without baking. Spread the mixture out in a 1cm layer on a baking tray lined with a silicone mat or baking paper using a spatula. The sponge must be large enough to cut 2 rings of 20cm. Bake it for 7 minutes, turn the tray and bake for another 3–5 minutes until golden brown. Cool on the tray.

2. For the kirsch syrup, put the water and sugar in a small pan and bring them to the boil. Cool the syrup for 15 minutes then add the kirsch or strawberry liqueur.

3. Turn the sponge over onto the work surface and gently peel off the silicone mat or baking paper. Place the ring over it and cut the 2 circles using a sharp knife on the outside of the ring.

4. Roll out the marzipan with icing sugar and cut a circle around the outside of the ring. Place the marzipan on a baking tray and caramelize it using a blowtorch.

5. Put the ring on a serving tray and place a circle of génoise in the base. Soak it in a little bit of kirsch syrup using a pastry brush.

6. Put the strawberries in a colander and wash them quickly under cold water. Drain and put them on a clean cloth to dry. Cut the bottoms off. Garnish the cake with half-strawberries around the inside of the ring and some whole strawberries inside the cake.

7. Make the pistachio cream: Soak the gelatine leaves in cold water for 10 minutes. Bring the caster sugar and water to the boil and, off the heat, add the pressed gelatine leaves. Whisk the cream with the pistachio paste and add the gelatine syrup when it starts to rise. The pistachio cream must double in size but still be runny enough to be poured over the strawberries.

8. Put the second circle of génoise on the top, soak it with the syrup and place the caramelized marzipan on top. Set in the fridge for 8 hours.

9. Before serving, blowtorch all the way around the ring to melt the edges and then remove the ring by lifting it up with a kitchen cloth. Decorate the cake with strawberries using some melted white chocolate to stick them onto the cake.

How to make chocolate shavings

Recipe for 150g of chocolate shavings made with tempered chocolate.

1. Chop 50g of dark chocolate (or one-third of total quantity) with a large knife.

2. Melt 100g of dark chocolate (or two-thirds of total quantity) in the microwave for 1 minute at a medium power. Stir with a spatula then repeat this step every 30 seconds until the chocolate is completely melted.

3. Add the chopped chocolate to the melted chocolate and stir with a spatula until it's melted. The chocolate is now tempered.

4. Spread out the chocolate in a thin layer on a work surface, and wait until it starts to crystallize.

5. Make the chocolate shavings using a scraper or a knife.

6. Store the chocolate shavings in a cool place (about 17°C).

Double chocolate and raspberry sponge

FRAMBOISIER AUX DEUX CHOCOLATS

A traditional framboisier is made with 2 layers of plain sponge and a vanilla cream composed of half buttercream and half crème pâtissière. I've adapted this classic recipe to make an all-chocolate and raspberry dessert.

Serves 12 / **Preparation time:** 20 + 40 minutes / **Baking time:** 10–12 minutes at 180°C/350°F/Gas Mark 4 / **Setting time in the fridge:** 8 hours / **You will need a 24 x 4.5cm hexagonal or a 20cm round cake tin**

INGREDIENTS

For the chocolate sponge
170g dark chocolate (70%), chopped
170g butter
4 medium eggs, separated
170g caster sugar
70g plain flour
7g baking powder
80g ground almonds
1 pinch of salt

For the white chocolate mousse
2 small gelatine leaves (3g)
120g white chocolate
200ml fresh double cream
1 vanilla pod (opened and scraped)
280ml fresh double cream

For the chocolate ganache
125g dark chocolate (64%), chopped
30g butter
60ml semi-skimmed or full fat milk
25ml fresh double cream

For the garnish
4 punnets of large raspberries

For the chocolate shavings (optional)
40g dark chocolate, melted
20g dark chocolate, chopped

1. For the chocolate sponge, melt the chocolate and the butter in the microwave for 30 seconds at a medium power. Stir with a spatula and repeat this step 3 or 4 times until both are melted. Cool for 10 minutes then add the egg yolks one at a time, followed by the sifted caster sugar, flour, baking powder and ground almonds. Whisk the egg whites with a pinch of salt to peak (see page 38). Incorporate a third with the chocolate mix, then incorporate the remaining two-thirds. Spread it out to 1cm thick over a tray lined with a silicone mat or baking paper. The sponge must be large enough to cut 2 hexagons of 24cm. Bake for 7 minutes at 180°C/350°F/Gas Mark 4, turn the tray and bake for another 3–5 minutes. Prick the sponge with a knife; if the blade comes out clean it's cooked. Cool on the mat.

2. Turn the sponge over onto the work surface and gently peel off the silicone mat or baking paper. Place the cake tin over it and cut 2 hexagons using a sharp knife on the outside of the tin.

3. Put the tin on a serving tray and place a hexagon of the chocolate sponge in the base. Garnish the cake with large raspberries.

4. To make the white chocolate mousse, follow the method on page 82 and pour it over the raspberries. Put the second hexagon on the top and press gently with the fingertips. Set in the fridge for 8 hours.

5. Make the chocolate shavings following the method on page 204, if using.

6. To make the chocolate ganache, melt the chocolate and butter in the microwave following the method in step 1. Then

add the cold milk and the cream in 3 or 4 batches. This will cool the temperature of the ganache. Put back in the microwave for an extra 20 seconds to warm it up and bring it back to 40°C (it must feel warm but not hot), which is a good temperature to use a ganache. Pour it over the cake and spread it out with a large pallet knife. Set in the fridge.

7. Half an hour before serving, blowtorch all the way around the hexagon frame to melt the edges of the cream and remove it by lifting it up with a kitchen cloth. Decorate the cake with white chocolate mousse, raspberries and chocolate shavings.

👍 GOOD TO KNOW

The chocolate sponge can be baked in a cake tin, then split in half and garnished with the set white chocolate mousse and fresh raspberries. Double the ingredients for the chocolate ganache, and cover the cake entirely.

Chestnut and pear charlotte

CHARLOTTE À LA CHÂTAIGNE ET AUX POIRES

Charlottes are light and melt in the mouth. The sponge biscuits can be soaked quickly in the pear poaching liquor, flavoured with a little dark rum if the dessert is intended for adults.

Serves 8 / **Preparation time:** 20 + 30 minutes
Baking time: 8–10 minutes at 160°C/325°F/Gas Mark 3 / **Setting time in the fridge:** 6 hours
You will need an 18cm high-sided round cake tin and a non-stick baking tray

INGREDIENTS
40 sponge fingers
  (see page 248)
butter, for greasing

For the poached pears
3 ripe Williams pears
500ml water
150g caster sugar
1 vanilla pod (opened
  and scraped)

For the chestnut mousse
4 small gelatine leaves
  (6g)
400g chestnut spread
350ml fresh double
  cream

*For the chocolate shavings
(optional)*
40g dark chocolate,
  melted
20g dark chocolate,
  chopped

1. Make the poached pears following the method on page 68.

2. Make the sponge fingers following the method on page 248. Cool on the tray.

3. Grease the mould with butter and line with baking paper.

4. For the chestnut mousse, soak the gelatine leaves in cold water for 10 minutes. Put the chestnut cream in a large bowl. Bring 50ml of cream to the boil and, off the heat, add the squeezed gelatine leaves. Pour the hot cream on top of the chestnut spread and stir with a spatula. Whisk the remaining 300ml of cream to a soft and runny whipped cream and fold it into the chestnut spread. The chestnut mousse must be soft and runny. Dice 4 poached pear halves and incorporate them to the mousse.

5. Line the bottom and the side of the mould with sponge fingers, placing the icing sugar sides in contact with the baking paper.

6. Pour in a third of the chestnut mousse and cover it with a layer of sponge fingers. Then add another third of mousse and a layer of sponge fingers. Finally, pour in the remaining mousse and a final layer of sponge fingers. Set in the fridge for a minimum of 6 hours.

7. Turn the mould upside down on a serving tray and help the charlotte to slide out by pulling gently on the baking paper.

8. Decorate the charlotte with sliced poached pears and chocolate shavings (see method page 204).

How to make a hazelnut dacquoise

1. Sift together the icing sugar, ground hazelnuts and plain flour.

2. Make a French meringue with the egg whites and the caster sugar. Whisk the egg whites at medium speed. When they start to rise, gradually add the caster sugar and beat until firm.

3. Pour in the sifted icing sugar, ground hazelnuts and plain flour on the top of the meringue in one go.

4. Gently combine the dry ingredients with the meringue using a spatula, without overworking it. Make a circular movement with the spatula in one hand, starting from the bottom upwards, and give the bowl a quarter turn with the other hand. Repeat these movements until the dacquoise mix is combined. Be careful not to overwork the dacquoise otherwise it will collapse.

5. Fill a piping bag fitted with a large nozzle.

6. Draw 3 circles of 20cm on baking paper and place them on 2 or 3 baking trays. Stick the baking paper to the tray with a little bit of dacquoise mix.

7. Pipe the dacquoise, starting from the middle of the circle, to form a snail shape up to the edge. Repeat this step with the 2 other circles.

8. Sprinkle the 3 dacquoises with chopped blanched hazelnuts and icing sugar.

9. Bake straight away for 14 minutes at 160°C/325°F/Gas Mark 3, then turn the tray and bake for another 2–4 minutes until evenly beige. Leave to cool down on the tray.

Hazelnut layer cake

DACQUOISE À LA NOISETTE

Originating from the south-west of France, this cake is named after the inhabitants of the town of Dax. Usually made with ground almonds, it can also be prepared with ground hazelnuts, ground pistachios or desiccated coconut and filled with different kinds of mousse. I recommend making this cake a day in advance; it will be moister and taste even better the following day.

Serves 8 / Preparation time: 1 hour / Baking time: 16–18 minutes at 160°C/325°F/Gas Mark 3
You will need 2or 3 baking trays (to pipe the 3 x 20cm sponge)

INGREDIENTS

For the homemade praline paste
150g blanched almonds
150g blanched hazelnuts
85g caster sugar
50ml water

For the hazelnut dacquoise sponge
175g ground hazelnuts
175g icing sugar
40g plain flour
7 egg whites (280g)
110g caster sugar
30g blanched hazelnuts, chopped
30g icing sugar, for dusting

For the praline mousse
2 small gelatine leaves (3g)
3 egg whites (120g)
230g caster sugar
75ml water
120g homemade or readymade praline paste (50% almonds, 50% hazelnuts)

1. Make the homemade praline paste following the method on page 194.

2. Make the hazelnut dacquoise following the method on page 210.

3. For the praline mousse, soak the gelatine leaves in cold water for 10 minutes. Make an Italian meringue following the method on page 38 and, off the heat, add the squeezed gelatine leaves to the syrup.

4. In a large bowl, whisk the praline paste and add a quarter of the Italian meringue with a whisk to soften the praline paste. Incorporate the rest of the meringue in one go using a spatula, making a circular movement from the bottom upwards with a spatula in one hand, and giving the bowl a quarter turn with the other. Repeat these movements until the praline mousse is evenly combined. Fill a piping bag fitted with a medium-size nozzle.

5. Peel off the baking paper from the 3 sponges and build up the dacquoise. Place 1 layer of sponge in the middle of a serving dish. Pipe over a layer of praline mousse and cover it with a second layer of sponge. Pipe a second layer of mousse and put the final layer of dacquoise sponge on top.

6. Keep in the fridge and dust with icing sugar before serving.

Chocolate and orange cake

REINE DE SABA À L'ORANGE

Rich and moist, this is a delicious and simple cake for all the family. You can also try it without orange, or swap the plain flour for potato flour to get what will probably be the best gluten-free cake you've ever tasted.

Serves 10 / **Preparation time:** 20 minutes / **Baking time:** 45–60 minutes at 160°C/325°F/Gas Mark 3 / **You will need a 20–24cm round cake tin**

INGREDIENTS
250g dark chocolate
  (70%), chopped
250g butter
6 medium eggs,
  separated
250g caster sugar
100g plain flour
10 g baking powder
120g ground almonds
1 medium orange (finely
  grated zest and juice)
1 pinch of salt

1. Grease the mould with butter and flour. Turn it over and knock it against the work surface to remove the excess flour.

2. Put the chocolate and the butter in a bowl. Melt them in the microwave, at a medium power for 1 minute, then check and stir with a spatula. Repeat this step every 30 seconds until both are melted. Or melt them slowly in a bain-marie (see page 24). Leave to cool to 35–40°C for 10–15 minutes.

3. Stir in the egg yolks one by one using a whisk. Add the caster sugar, plain flour, baking powder and ground almonds in one go, then add the zest and the juice of the orange.

4. Whisk the 6 egg whites with a pinch of salt to peak (see page 38). Incorporate a third into the chocolate mix to lighten it, followed by the last two-thirds, making a circular movement from the bottom upwards with a spatula in one hand, and giving a quarter turn to the bowl with the other. Repeat this step until the mix is combined without overworking it.

5. Fill the cake tin and bake the cake straight away. Prick the cake with the blade of a knife; if it comes out clean it's cooked. Cool on a wire rack.

Black Forest gateau

FORÊT-NOIRE

Originally from Germany, the Black Forest gateau is also very popular in Alsace at the frontier between France and Germany, and everywhere in France. Be generous with the griottines; they give the cake its unique flavour.

Serves 12 / **Preparation time:** 20 + 40 minutes / **Baking time:** 30–40 minutes at 160°C/325°F/Gas Mark 3 / **Resting time in fridge:** 15 + 20 minutes
You will need a 20–22cm round cake tin

INGREDIENTS

For the chocolate génoise
150g plain flour
30g cocoa powder
6 medium eggs
185g caster sugar

For the chocolate shavings
100g dark chocolate, melted
50g dark chocolate, chopped

For the kirsch garnish
600g Chantilly cream (2 x recipe on page 34)
200g griottines (morello cherries preserved in kirsch)

For the chocolate ganache
125g dark chocolate (64%), chopped
30g butter
60ml semi-skimmed or full fat milk
25ml fresh double cream

1. Sift the plain flour with the cocoa powder and make the chocolate génoise sponge following the method on page 24. Bake and cool for 1 hour on a wire rack.

2. Make the chocolate shavings (page 204).

3. Drain the kirsch cherries and place them on kitchen paper to dry. Set aside the kirsch liqueur to soak the chocolate génoise. Cut the cherries in half.

4. Make the Chantilly cream following the method on page 34 and keep it in the fridge. Turn the chocolate génoise upside down and split it sideways into 3 equal parts.

5. Soak the inside of the bottom part with kirsch liqueur using a pastry brush. Spread over a layer of Chantilly cream (1cm thick), divide the cherry halves and push them into the cream.

6. Put the middle section of the cake back on top of the cream, and repeat step 5.

7. Soak the inside of the top part of the génoise and place it on top of the cake. Press gently on it with the palm of your hand to level it out. Remove the excess Chantilly cream around the side of the cake using a spatula and place it in the fridge for 15 minutes.

8. For the chocolate ganache, melt the chocolate and the butter in the microwave for 30 seconds, at a medium power. Stir with a spatula and repeat this step 3 or 4 times until both are melted. Or melt them over a bain-marie (see page 24). Then add the cold milk and the cream in 3 or 4 batches. This will cool the temperature of the ganache. Return to the microwave for another 20 seconds to warm it up and bring it back to 40°C (it must feel warm but not hot).

9. Spread out the ganache on the top of the cake and level it out using a long spatula or knife. Remove roughly the excess of ganache from the side of the cake. Set in the fridge for 20 minutes.

10. Spread out a thin layer of Chantilly cream all around the cake, and decorate it with chocolate shavings. Use the leftover Chantilly cream, chocolate shavings and griottines to decorate the top of the Black Forest gateau. Keep it in the fridge and remove it 1 hour before serving.

CHAPTER 9

Sweet treats

GOURMANDISES

Dark chocolate and lemon madeleines

MADELEINES AU CITRON ET AU CHOCOLAT NOIR

This recipe is my grown-up version of the classic madeleines. You can also try them plain with 1 teaspoon of vanilla extract instead of the lemon zest. Children love them.

Serves 8 (24 madeleines) / **Preparation time:** 15 minutes / **Resting time in the fridge:** 4 hours (or overnight) / **Baking time:** 8–10 minutes at 190°C/375°F/Gas Mark 5
You will need a silicone mould for 9 or 12 madeleines

INGREDIENTS
250g melted butter, warm
250g plain flour
1 pinch of salt
8g baking powder
5 medium eggs
250g caster sugar
thinly grated zest of 1 lemon
100g dark chocolate, chopped

1. Slowly melt the butter in a pan or in the microwave.

2. Sift together the plain flour, salt and baking powder.

3. In a large bowl, whisk the eggs, caster sugar and lemon zest for 1 minute. Add the sifted powders all at the same time and mix until it has an even consistency. Finally, incorporate slowly the warm melted butter into the mix.

4. Cover the madeleine mix with cling film in contact and rest in the fridge for a minimum of 4 hours, or overnight if possible. It will help the madeleines to rise during baking.

5. Grease the madeleines moulds with soft butter, and fill them two-thirds full using a tablespoon or a piping bag.

6. Bake straight away until golden brown and turn them out while still warm. Put them back in the mould on their sides to cool.

7. Melt the dark chocolate in the microwave at medium power for 1 minute, then check and stir with a spatula. Repeat this step every 30 seconds until the chocolate is melted. Alternatively, melt it slowly in a bain-marie (see page 24). Dip the bottom of the madeleines into the chocolate and place them in the fridge for 10 minutes to allow them to crystallize. Enjoy the madeleines at room temperature.

Apricot financiers

FINANCIERS À L'ABRICOT

Financiers are small individual rectanglar cakes generally eaten in France at the end of a meal with coffee. They are usually made with ground almonds, and can also be flavoured with griottines (morello cherries preserved in kirsch), lemon zest and blueberries, rhubarb or chocolate. Ground hazelnuts or a mix of ground almonds and ground pistachios can be used instead of the ground almonds.

Serves 12 / **Preparation time:** 25 minutes / **Resting time:** 1 hour in the fridge
Baking time: 15 minutes at 160°C/325°F/Gas Mark 3
You will need a silicone mould for 20 small financiers (2 x 4cm)

INGREDIENTS
170g butter
250g icing sugar
135g ground almonds
55g plain flour
5 egg whites (200g)

For the garnish
50g almond batons
8 fresh apricots, diced

1. In a pan, at a low heat, melt the butter and continue cooking for a few minutes until it becomes light brown (*beurre noisette*). Leave it cool for 20 minutes.

2. Sift the icing sugar, ground almonds and flour in a bowl. Add the cold melted brown butter and 1 egg white, and stir with a whisk. Then add the rest of the egg whites two at a time.

3. Fill a piping bag and rest the mixture in the fridge for 1 hour before baking.

4. Brush the silicone moulds with soft butter and fill them (two-thirds full). Garnish each financier with 3 pieces of diced apricot and a few almond batons. Bake until golden but not too dark otherwise they will be too dry and cool in the moulds.

5. Repeat step 4 a few times to finish off the mix. The financier mix can be kept in the fridge for 3 days.

Cannelés

Originating in Bordeaux, these little cakes can be served as a dessert or at the end of a meal with coffee. The condensed milk is not a traditional ingredient but more a modern evolution of this recipe. I personally find they taste better this way.

Serves 6 / **Preparation time:** 30 minutes / **Resting time in the fridge:** 24 hours
Baking time: 25–30 minutes at 170°C/325°F/Gas Mark 3
You will need 12 small copper moulds or a silicone mould for 12 small cannelés

INGREDIENTS

225ml full fat milk
2 vanilla pods (opened and scraped)
1 medium egg
1 egg yolk
150g caster sugar
100ml condensed milk
80g plain flour
25g dark rum
25g hot melted butter
50g soft butter, for greasing

1. Bring the full fat milk with the vanilla pods to the boil and leave to cool down at room temperature.

2. In a large bowl, whisk together the egg, yolk and caster sugar, then add the condensed milk followed by the flour and the dark rum.

3. Add the cold milk and vanilla mix, and finally the hot melted butter. Pass the cannelés mix through a very fine sieve and store in the fridge for 24 hours.

4. The following day, grease the copper or silicone moulds with butter using a pastry brush.

5. Whisk the cannelés mix for 1 minute before use. Fill the moulds using a jug or a piping bag, leaving a 0.5cm gap at the top of the moulds, and start baking at 170°C/325°F/Gas Mark 3 for 10 minutes. The cannelés tend to rise above their moulds. After 10 minutes, remove the tray from the oven and prick the cannelés with a knife tip to make them collapse inside their moulds. Continue baking for another 15–20 minutes. They are cooked when dark and caramelized on the outside. Cool them out of their moulds on a cooling rack. Repeat step 4 and 5 with any remaining mix.

👍 GOOD TO KNOW

Copper moulds provide a better-looking and crispier result. Before their first use, the copper moulds should be brushed in and out with butter, put in the oven for 20 minutes at 250°C/480°F/Gas Mark 9, then cleaned while they are still hot. They should then never be washed again, only flashed in the oven for 5 minutes and wiped clean with a kitchen cloth. Silicone moulds work just fine, however, and you can get a similar result by flashing the cannelés in a hot oven for 4 minutes out of their moulds.

How to make macaroons

There are 2 methods for making macaroons: with a French meringue, which is the traditional one, or with an Italian meringue, which is the modern way used by most pastry chefs and bakers. They are less fragile and more practical to use. I was taught the traditional way when I was 18, and ever since I've been using a French meringue in all my macaroon mixes. The macaroon shells are soft and chewy and can be filled and eaten right away, while macaroon shells made with an Italian meringue are hard, and need to be filled and placed in the fridge for 24–48 hours to moisten.

1. Blitz together the icing sugar and the ground almonds/hazelnuts in a food processor for a few seconds then pass the mix through a sieve.

2. Using an electric mixer at medium speed, whisk the egg whites, caster sugar and food colouring (according to the recipe) until a stiff peak forms (see page 38).

3. Pour the egg whites over the sifted powders and start mixing gently with a spatula.

4. Combine the powders with the egg whites until you get a thick, slightly shiny and almost runny paste. It's important to stop working the mix when it starts to shine at the risk of overworking it. When you stop working the mix, it must flatten out almost completely on its own in the bowl, within 30 seconds. If it's very runny and flattens out right away, the egg whites are overworked. And if it doesn't flatten out almost completely after 30 seconds it's underworked.

5. Fill a piping bag fitted with a medium-size nozzle.

6. On a tray lined with baking paper, pipe the macaroons in staggered rows. Stick the paper to the tray with a little bit of macaroon mix or put a small mould in each corner of the tray to stop the fan from blowing it away.

7. Rest the macaroons for 1 hour at room temperature, until their tops start to dry and form a crust, before baking.

8. Bake the macaroons on the top shelf of the oven (to protect them from the fan) for 7 minutes at 150°/300°F/Gas Mark 2, then turn the tray and bake for another 3–4 minutes according to the size of your macaroons. Cool on the tray.

9. Fill the macaroons: pick 2 macaroons of the same size, place a little bit of cream inside one of them, put the second one on top of it and press gently. Place in the fridge and remove 10–20 minutes before serving.

1. You can judge the quality of your macaroon mix when it is piped onto the baking tray: if it doesn't flatten out evenly, it is underworked; if it spreads out excessively, it's overworked.

2. The perfect macaroon must be chewy inside: if they are dry they have been overcooked. If some humidity stains appear on their tops while cooling, they are undercooked and require an extra 2 minutes in the oven.

3. The macaroon shells can be frozen without filling.

4. Dry macaroons can be 'saved' by filling them with the cream and keeping them in the fridge for 24 hours. They will absorb the humidity of the cream and become chewy.

Raspberry macaroons

MACARONS À LA FRAMBOISE

I always try not to use any food colouring in pâtisserie. However, macaroons are the only exception. The colour of the macaroon shell is meant to represent its flavour. For example, a deep-pink colour is used to represent a fresh raspberry macaroon.

Makes approximately 35 / **Preparation time:** 20 + 10 minutes
Resting time at room temperature: 1 hour / **Baking time:** 9–11 minutes at 150°C/300F/Gas Mark 2
You will need a baking tray covered with baking paper (30 x 40cm)

INGREDIENTS
125g ground almonds
225g icing sugar
3 egg whites (120g)
20g caster sugar
red food colouring

For the raspberry cream
200ml fresh double
   cream
30g caster sugar
60g fresh raspberries

1. Make the macaroons following the method on page 226.

2. For the raspberry cream, whisk the cream with the caster sugar until it starts to thicken, then add the fresh raspberries and keep whisking until the mixture is stiff. The raspberry cream tends to loosen up in the fridge after a few hours and might need to be whisked again.

3. Fill a piping bag fitted with a medium-size nozzle with the raspberry cream and fill the macaroons. Keep in the fridge and allow 10 minutes at room temperature to warm up before serving.

Lemon macaroons

MACARONS AU CITRON

All kinds of extravagant flavours of macaroons can now be found in pâtisserie shops. But sometimes a classic and simple flavour like lemon together with a crispy almond shell is just right.

Makes approximately 35 / **Preparation time:** 20 + 10 minutes
Resting time at room temperature: 1 hour / **Baking time:** 9–11 minutes at 150°C/300F/Gas Mark 2
You will need a baking tray covered with baking paper (30 x 40cm)

INGREDIENTS
For the macaroons
125g ground almonds
225g icing sugar
3 egg whites (120g)
20g caster sugar
yellow food colouring

For the lemon cream
300ml fresh double
  cream
50g caster sugar
1 grated lemon zest
60ml lemon juice

1. Make the macaroons following the method on page 226.

2. For the lemon cream, whisk the cream with the caster sugar and lemon zest until it starts to thicken, then add the lemon juice and keep whisking until it's stiff.

3. Fill a piping bag fitted with a medium-size nozzle with the lemon cream and fill the macaroons. Store in the fridge and allow 10 minutes at room temperature to warm up before serving.

GOOD TO KNOW

The classic macaroons are made of ground almonds and food colouring. The flavour of the filling (cream, ganache or jam) and the colour of the shells will determine the flavour of the macaroons.

Hazelnut and milk chocolate macaroons

MACARONS À LA NOISETTE ET AU CHOCOLAT AU LAIT

Macaroon shells made with ground hazelnuts instead of ground almonds are something a little bit more unusual. It's a completely different taste that I recommend you to try.

Makes approximately 35 / **Preparation time:** 20 + 10 minutes / **Resting time in the fridge:** 2 hours / **Resting time at room temperature:** 1 hour / **Baking time:** 9–11 minutes at 150°C/300F/Gas Mark 2 / **You will need a baking tray covered with baking paper (30 x 40cm)**

INGREDIENTS

For the milk chocolate mousse
100g milk chocolate, chopped
100ml fresh double cream
250ml fresh double cream, softly whipped

For the hazelnut macaroons
125g ground hazelnuts
225g icing sugar
3 egg whites (120g)
20g caster sugar

1. For the milk chocolate mousse, place the chopped chocolate in a large bowl. Bring the cream to the boil and pour it over the chocolate, stirring with a spatula until it melts. Cool at room temperature for 10 minutes, then fold in the whipped cream. Set in the fridge for a minimum of 2 hours (see the white chocolate and vanilla mousse method on page 82).

2. Make the macaroons following the method on page 226.

3. Fill a piping bag fitted with a medium-size nozzle with the milk chocolate mousse and fill the macaroons. Store in the fridge and allow 10 minutes at room temperature to warm up before serving.

👍 GOOD TO KNOW

The macaroons can be made with various kinds of nut powders (almond, hazelnut, pistachio, peanut, pecan). The texture and the look of the macaroons may change a little according to the fat content in each nut powder.

Flaked almond tuiles

TUILES AUX AMANDES EFFILÉES

Delicious and crispy, these flaked almonds tuiles can be served with a chocolate mousse (page 62), vanilla ice cream (page 26) or crème brûlée (page 180). They are also perfect with a nice cup of tea or coffee.

Serves 8 (25 tuiles) / **Preparation time:** 15 minutes / **Resting time in the fridge:** 4 hours
Baking time: 12–15 minutes at 150°C/300°F/Gas Mark 2 / **You will need 2 baking trays covered with a silicone mat or 2 non-stick baking trays (30 x 40cm)**

INGREDIENTS
25g soft butter
125g caster sugar
40g plain flour
50ml fresh orange juice,
  sieved
65g flaked almonds

1. Using an electric mixer fitted with a paddle, mix the butter, caster sugar and flour until it has an even consistency. Then slowly incorporate the fresh orange juice.

2. By hand with a spatula, stir in the flaked almonds and then rest the mixture in the fridge for a minimum of 4 hours before use.

3. On a non-stick baking tray or a tray lined with a silicone mat, place 12 teaspoonfuls of mix in staggered rows, separated by 15cm. Flatten them out with your fingertips and form them into a round shape. Bake on a high shelf in the oven (above the fan) for 10 minutes, then turn the tray and continue cooking for another 3–5 minutes until golden brown.

4. Cool the tuiles on the tray for 2 minutes then lift them up with a plastic scraper and shape them around a rolling pin. Store in an airtight container.

5. Repeat steps 3 and 4 until all the mixture has been used.

Dark chocolate florentines

Originally from Brittany in northern France, these biscuits can also be coated with milk or white chocolate. I recommend you enjoy them with a strong coffee at the end of a meal or as an afternoon treat.

Serves 8 / **Preparation time:** 15 + 15 minutes
Baking time: 14–16 minutes at 150°C/300°F/Gas Mark 2
You will need 2 baking trays covered with a silicone mat or 2 non-stick baking trays (30 x 40cm)

INGREDIENTS
100g caster sugar
50g plain flour
120ml fresh double
  cream
25g runny honey
15g butter
125g flaked almonds
60g orange peel
60g lemon peel

For the chocolate icing
120g dark chocolate
  (70%), chopped
10g butter

1. Mix the plain flour with the caster sugar and pass though a very fine sieve.

2. Put the cream, honey and butter in a pan and bring it slowly to the boil. Off the heat, incorporate the sifted flour and caster sugar all in one go, stir with a whisk and bring the mix back to the boil. Remove the pan from the heat and use a spatula to incorporate the flaked almonds, orange and lemon peel.

3. On 2 trays lined with a silicone mat or 2 non-stick baking trays, place small quantities of mix in staggered rows using a teaspoon (metal rings can be used to control the shape of the florentines while baking). Flatten them out using your fingertips and bake for 10 minutes, then turn the tray and continue baking for 4–6 extra minutes until golden brown. Cool on the tray (the metal rings must be removed while they are still warm, with a knife tip).

4. To make the chocolate icing, put the chocolate and butter in a bowl and melt in the microwave at a medium power for 1 minute, then check and stir with a spatula. Repeat this step every 30 seconds until both are melted. Alternatively, melt them slowly in a bain-marie (see page 24).

5. Turn the florentines upside down and spread over a teaspoon of chocolate icing. Decorate them using a fork or a decorating comb and leave the chocolate to set at room temperature.

6. The dark chocolate florentines will keep for a few days in an airtight container.

Bretons biscuits

GALETTES BRETONNES

Light and crispy, these are great served with a crème caramel (page 182) or bavarois (page 186). Salted butter is traditionally used in Brittany, but 130g of unsalted butter and 2g of salt can be used instead.

Makes approximately 25 / **Preparation time:** 10 minutes / **Resting time in the fridge:** 2 hours
Baking time: 10–11 minutes at 170°C/325°F/Gas Mark 3
You will need 2 baking trays covered with a silicone mat or 2 non-stick baking trays (30 x 40cm)

INGREDIENTS
130g soft salted butter
135g caster sugar
230g plain flour
7g baking powder
1 medium egg

1. Cream the butter with the caster sugar using an electric mixer fitted with a paddle, or in a large bowl with a spatula.

2. Add the plain flour and baking powder, and work the mix until it has a sandy texture. Incorporate the egg.

3. Roll the biscuit mixture into a sausage shape 4cm in diameter, wrap in cling film and place in the fridge for 2 hours.

4. Cut the biscuit mix into 1cm wide slices. Put them on 2 non-stick baking trays or 2 trays covered with a silicone mat in staggered rows, 5cm apart. Bake for 8 minutes, then turn the trays, and continue baking for another 2–3 minutes until golden. Cool on the trays.

Nini's sablés biscuits

SABLÉS DE NINI

My sister Stéphanie, or Nini, used to make these biscuits all the time when we were teenagers. Dense and crumbly, these sablés could be compared to shortbread. They are ideal for lunch boxes.

Makes approximately 25 / **Preparation time:** 10 minutes / **Resting time in the fridge:** 2 hours
Baking time: 14–16 minutes at 170°C/325°F/Gas Mark 3
You will need 2 baking trays covered with a silicone mat or 2 non-stick baking trays (30 x 40cm)

INGREDIENTS
250g plain flour
125g caster sugar
1 pinch salt
125g soft butter
1 medium egg
100g demerara sugar

1. Work the flour, caster sugar, salt and butter into a sandy texture by hand or use an electric mixer fitted with a paddle. Incorporate the egg.

2. Roll the biscuit mix into a sausage shape, 5cm in diameter. Sprinkle the demerara sugar on the work surface and roll the biscuit mix across it. Wrap in cling film and place in the fridge for 2 hours.

3. Cut the biscuit mix into 1cm thick slices. Put them on the non-stick baking trays (or 2 baking trays covered with a silicone mat) in staggered rows, 5cm apart. Bake for 12 minutes then turn the tray and continue baking for another 2–4 minutes until golden. Cool on the tray.

Finger biscuits

I can't resist giving you the literal translation of Langues-de-chat: it's 'cat's tongue'. I will leave you to imagine the silly games played by children in France. These finger biscuits work well served with a crème brûlée (page 180), vanilla ice cream (page 26) or fresh fruit salad.

Makes approximately 30 / **Preparation time:** 15 minutes
Baking time: 5–6 minutes at 200°C/400°F/Gas Mark 6
You will need 2 baking trays covered with a silicone mat (30 x 40cm)

INGREDIENTS
60g soft butter
40g caster sugar
70g plain flour
1 medium egg
1 teaspoon vanilla
   extract

1. In a bowl, mix the soft butter with the caster sugar using a spatula. Add the flour, then the egg, vanilla extract and combine. This can also be done in a food processor or an electric mixer fitted with a paddle.

2. Fill a piping bag fitted with a small nozzle (or use a teaspoon).

3. On 2 trays lined with a silicone mat, pipe the finger biscuits in 6cm-long lines, in staggered rows, with 3cm gaps in between.

4. Bake for 4 minutes and then turn the trays and bake for an extra minute or 2. Cool on the trays.

Rolled biscuits

CIGARETTES RUSSES

Light and crispy, rolled biscuits are ideal served with a dark chocolate and orange mousse (page 184) or vanilla ice cream (page 26).

Makes approximately 40 / **Preparation time:** 15 minutes / **Resting time in the fridge:** 1 hour
Baking time: 5–6 minutes at 160°C/325°F/Gas Mark 3 / **You will need 2 baking trays covered with a silicone mat or 2 non-stick baking trays (30 x 40cm)**

INGREDIENTS
100g butter
100g icing sugar
75g plain flour
3 egg whites (120g)

1. Put the butter and icing sugar in a food processor and mix until well combined.

2. Add all of the flour and process for 1 minute. Scrape the inside of the bowl with a spatula.

3. Finally, incorporate the egg whites one at a time, without overworking the mix. Rest in the fridge for 1 hour.

4. On 2 non-stick baking trays or trays lined with a silicone mat, spread about 12 teaspoonfuls of the mixture, using the back of the teaspoon to shape. Try to be as round and regular as possible.

5. One tray at a time, bake the biscuits for 4 minutes then turn the tray in the oven and bake for another 1 or 2 minutes. The rolled biscuits must be golden brown on the edges and still a little pale in the middle.

6. Peel one biscuit off the tray using a plastic scraper. Turn it over on the tray and roll the cigarette starting at one end. Press on the cigarette lightly to seal the joint.

7. Repeat step 6 for each cigarette. As they start to cool, put the tray back in the oven for 1 minute to warm up the biscuits and finish rolling them.

👍 GOOD TO KNOW

The biscuits can also be rolled around a thin wooden stick following the same method.

French meringues

MERINGUES FRANÇAISES

Crispy and melt-in-the-mouth, French meringues can be served as a dessert with fresh strawberries and Chantilly cream (page 34) or can be enjoyed on their own.

Serves 12 / **Preparation time:** 15 minutes
Baking time: 30–40 minutes at 110°C/225°F/Gas Mark ¼
You will need 2 baking trays covered with a silicone mat or baking paper (30 x 40cm)

INGREDIENTS
4 egg whites (150g)
140g caster sugar
140g icing sugar
30g flaked almonds
 (optional)
20g icing sugar, to dust
 (optional)

1. Whisk the egg whites with the caster sugar to firm peaks (see page 38) using an electric mixer at medium speed. It will take about 10 minutes.

2. Sift the icing sugar and use a spatula to incorporate it in one addition with the egg whites, without overworking it.

3. Fill a piping bag fitted with a large fluted nozzle and pipe the French meringues onto 2 trays lined with baking paper or silicone mat.

4. Sprinkle the meringues with flaked almonds and icing sugar, if using.

5. Bake slowly for 30–40 minutes according to their size. Leave them to cool down and dry inside the switched-off oven for 4 hours.

👍 GOOD TO KNOW

The same recipe can be used to make chewy pavlovas. The baking time will be 25 minutes for individual pavlovas and 40 minutes at 120°C/250°F/Gas Mark ½ for a large one.

Sponge fingers

BISCUITS À LA CUILLÈRE

Sponge fingers are used in the making of charlottes (page 208) and tiramisu, sometimes soaked in a syrup. Very light and butter free, they are also delicious on their own and make a successful snack for the lunch box.

Makes 40 / **Preparation time:** 20 minutes
Baking time: 8–10 minutes at 160°C/325°F/Gas Mark 3
You will need 2 baking trays covered with a silicone mat (30 x 40cm)

INGREDIENTS
3 eggs, separated (120g)
70g caster sugar
75g plain flour, sifted
50g icing sugar, to dust

1. Whisk the egg whites with the caster sugar to a stiff meringue (page 38) using an electric mixer at medium speed.

2. Reduce the speed of the mixer to low and incorporate the egg yolks to the meringue without overworking the mix. Then by hand, fold in the flour in 3 additions, using a spatula.

3. Fill a piping bag fitted with a large nozzle.

4. On 2 trays lined with a silicone mat, pipe the sponge fingers in 5cm lines, in staggered rows, leaving 3cm gaps between each.

5. Dust the sponge fingers with icing sugar and let them melt at room temperature for 15 minutes. Dust the sponge fingers a second time before baking until evenly light beige. Cool on a tray. The melted icing sugar will form the sugar pearls you can see on top of the biscuits.

Heart-shaped biscuits

PALMIERS

Heart-shaped biscuits are made of caramelized puff pastry. This recipe is a good way to use up small pieces of unused puff pastry. Enjoy the palmiers on their own or served with floating islands (page 178) or lemon soufflé (page 188).

Makes approximately 20 / **Preparation time:** 40 + 15 minutes / **Resting time in the fridge:** 2¹/₂ hours + 15 minutes / **Baking time:** 10–15 minutes at 170°C/325°F/Gas Mark 3
You will need 2 non-stick baking trays

INGREDIENTS
300g puff pastry or
   chocolate puff pastry
   (see pages 12 and
   112)
50g icing sugar
1 beaten egg

1. Make the puff pastry following the method on page 12. This step can be done the day before.

2. Roll out the puff pastry with some icing sugar into a 20 x 30cm rectangle, 5mm thick. Icing sugar is used instead of flour to stop the pastry from sticking to the work surface. Some of it will be absorbed by the pastry, and caramelize during baking.

3. Remove the excess icing sugar with a brush or your fingertips and place one of the short sides of the rectangle in front of you. Brush 2 bands 7cm wide with a very thin layer of beaten egg (at the top and at the bottom of the rectangle) and fold them towards the middle, leaving a 2cm gap in the centre. Brush the bottom section with a very thin layer of egg and fold it over the top section. You now have a 20 x 8cm widthways rectangle in front of you.

4. Cut the 20cm rectangle into 20 pieces 1cm wide and put them on their side on a non-stick tray, in staggered rows, 10cm apart. The folds are now appearing and you can start to see a flat heat-shape form. Place in the fridge for 15 minutes before baking. The heart-shape form will appear during the baking of the sugar-coated puff pastry.

5. Bake the biscuits for 10 minutes, turn the trays and continue to bake for another 2–5 minutes, until the biscuits are golden brown but not too dark.

Crisp cinnamon biscuits

ARLETTES À LA CANNELLE

This recipe will allow you to use up all the puff pastry trimmings. Serve the crisp cinnamon biscuit with crème caramel (page 182) or dark chocolate and orange mousse (page 184).

Makes approximately 30 / **Preparation time:** 20 minutes / **Resting time in the freezer:** 2 hours
Resting time in the fridge: 30 minutes / **Baking time:** 10–14 minutes at 180°C/350°F/Gas Mark 4
You will need 2 non-stick baking trays

INGREDIENTS
200g puff pastry or puff pastry trimmings (see page 12, piled up carefully on top of each other)
20g butter
50g icing sugar
$^1/_2$ teaspoon ground cinnamon

1. Make the puff pastry following the method on page 12. This can be done the day before.

2. Melt the butter in a pan. Roll out the puff pastry into a rectangle, 2mm thick, and brush it with butter. Roll the pastry into a sausage shape, and put it in the freezer for 2 hours.

3. Mix the icing sugar with the cinnamon using a fork and spread it out on a plate.

4. Remove the puff pastry from the freezer and cut it with a sharp knife into 3mm slices.

5. Coat each slice with cinnamon icing sugar and roll them out very thinly in order to get a waffle-thin pastry, 10cm in diameter, using as much cinnamon icing sugar as needed.

6. Place the crisp cinnamon biscuits between 2 sheets of baking paper, then between 2 baking trays to keep them flat, and put them in the fridge for 30 minutes. Bake for 8 minutes then turn the trays and bake for another 2–4 minutes until they are golden brown. Cool on a wire rack.

Acknowledgements

To my sister Isabelle Valette. It's been an incredible journey, and a very long one too! It has been three years since that extraordinary evening (with just a little bit too much red wine) on your Oslo terrace when it all started. Isa, thank you for making me understand that the only limits are in our minds and for being there for me every step of the way.

To Annabelle Coelho and Greg Bartholomew. Thank you Annabelle for your constant support and encouragement when I most needed it! You're an amazing friend. Thank you both for your time and advice, and for patiently going over the manuscript in a very short period of time.

A special thank you to Miranda and Pontus Carminger, Ockenden Manor's owners and my sponsors, for financing the photo shoots and allowing me to use the facilities to test the recipes, as well as organise the photo sessions. Thank you for believing in me at an early stage of the book and making the adventure possible. A special thanks to Stephen Crane, Ockenden Manor's head chef, for creating inventive schedules that allowed me to both write and work at the same time. A really big thanks to Mark Charker, the junior sous-chef (and my number one), Alasdair Mulvey and Jack Amstrong for covering for me in pastry. Thank you Adam Smith, Ockenden Manor's manager, for your guidance, support and advice. Thank you Stuart Dolby (assistant restaurant manager), William Spalla (restaurant manager), Vincent Fayat (sous-chef), Sue Maxted and Tiffani Thompson for your help during the photo shoots. A big thanks to all my colleagues for tasting the recipes and giving me feedback. I loved sharing that experience with you all.

Thank you Lisa Devlin, an amazing and gifted photographer, for your wonderful pictures and designing skills. Working with you was inspiring on so many levels and really fun too. The book would not have looked the same without you. Thanks Poppy Bartholomew for your legal expertise.

A huge thanks to my publishers, Nikki Read and Giles Lewis for making my dream of writing a cookbook in English a reality! I would also like to thank everyone at How To Books and Constable & Robinson: Jo Stansall, Nicki Gyopari, Ian Hughes and everyone who worked on this book.

To my family, my supporting team. Thank you Maman for all the great inspiration, pastry talks and for sending me some pieces of France and home for the photos shoots. Thanks Papa for your strategic advice, and my sisters Stéphanie Valette and Emilie Valette, for taking so many nice family pictures. Thanks Øyvind Remme and Boris Pageaux for the IT support at key moments and, a special merci to Øyvind for making great dinners for Isa and me when we needed to hold it together. A big thanks to Angélique Salvagnac, Marie-Paule Salvagnac, Guy Salvagnac, Jean-Philippe Salvagnac, Thibault Chaudières, Eric Chirio and my very young commis chef twins Antoine and Clara Chirio, together with Paul Chirio for your help during the photo shoots in France.

This book has been a family affair! I'm so glad that you are all a part of this adventure, there is a little of each of you in it. *De tout cœur, merci.*

Index